SUSTAINING THE PEACE AFTER CIVIL WAR

T. David Mason

December 2007

This manuscript was funded by the U.S. Army War College External Research Associates Program. Information on this program is available on our website, *www.StrategicStudiesInstitute. army.mil*, at the Publishing button.

*****

Comments pertaining to this report are invited and should be forwarded to: Director, Strategic Studies Institute, U.S. Army War College, 122 Forbes Ave, Carlisle, PA 17013-5244.

*****

All Strategic Studies Institute (SSI) publications are available on the SSI homepage for electronic dissemination. Hard copies of this report also may be ordered from our homepage. SSI's homepage address is: *www.StrategicStudiesInstitute.army.mil*.

*****

The Strategic Studies Institute publishes a monthly e-mail newsletter to update the national security community on the research of our analysts, recent and forthcoming publications, and upcoming conferences sponsored by the Institute. Each newsletter also provides a strategic commentary by one of our research analysts. If you are interested in receiving this newsletter, please subscribe on our homepage at *www.StrategicStudiesInstitute.army. mil/newsletter/*.

ISBN 1-58487-331-0

FOREWORD

Since the end of World War II, there have been four times as many civil wars as interstate wars. For a small subset of nations, *civil war is a chronic condition*: about half of the civil war nations have had at least two and as many as six conflicts. The author of this monograph, Dr. David Mason, seeks to spell out what social science research can tell us about how civil wars end and what predicts whether (and when) they will recur. After summarizing research on what factors define the risk set of nations that are susceptible to civil war onset, he presents an analytical framework that has been used, first, to explain and predict how civil wars end — whether in a government victory, a rebel victory, or a negotiated settlement — and, second, whether the peace will last following the termination of the conflict (or, alternatively, the nation will experience a relapse into civil war). Research suggests that the outcome of the previous civil war — whether it ended in a government victory, a rebel victory or a negotiated settlement — as well as the duration and deadliness of the conflict, affect the durability of the peace after civil war.

The international community can reduce the prospects for a resumption of armed conflict by 1) introducing peacekeeping forces, 2) investing in economic development and reconstruction, and 3) establishing democratic political institutions tailored to the configuration of ethnic and religious cleavages in the society. The author closes by applying these propositions in an analysis of the civil war in Iraq: What can be done to bring the Iraq conflict to an earlier, less destructive, and more stable conclusion?

The Strategic Studies Institute is pleased to publish this work as part of our External Research Associates Program.

DOUGLAS C. LOVELACE, JR.
Director
Strategic Studies Institute

BIOGRAPHICAL SKETCH OF THE AUTHOR

T. DAVID MASON is is the Johnie Christian Family Peace Professor at the University of North Texas and Editor in Chief of *International Studies Quarterly*. He has held faculty positions at Mississippi State University (1981-92) and the University of Memphis (1992-2002). He is the author of *Caught in the Crossfire: Revolution, Repression, and the Rational Peasant* (Rowman & Littlefield 2004) and co-editor (with James Meernik) of *Conflict Prevention and Peace-building in Post-War Societies: Sustaining the Peace* (Routledge, 2006) as well over 40 book chapters and journal articles in such journals as *American Political Science Review, Journal of Politics, Political Research Quarterly, International Studies Quarterly, Journal of Conflict Resolution, Journal of Peace Research, Terrorism and Political Violence, Social Science Quarterly, Public Choice,* and *Comparative Political Studies.* Dr. Mason holds a Ph.D. in Political Science from the University of Georgia.

SUMMARY

Without exception, every widely used data set on civil wars indicates that once a civil war ends in a nation, that nation is at risk of experiencing another one at a later date. I will present a conceptual framework that allows us to identify the factors that make the post-civil war peace more likely to break down into a resumption of civil war.

Alternatively, this framework will allow us to point to those factors that make the post-civil war peace more durable. Many of these factors are policy-manipulable variables: there are policy tools at the disposal of the international community that can inoculate a post-civil war nation against the prospects of a relapse into renewed civil war. The analytical framework that informs the analysis suggests that the outcome of the previous civil war—whether it ended in a government victory, a rebel victory, or a negotiated settlement—as well as the duration and deadliness of the civil war affect the durability of the peace after civil war. In addition, characteristics of the post-civil war environment—the extent of democracy, the level of economic development, and the degree of ethnic fractionalization—also affect the durability of the peace.

Finally, there is a set of policy interventions at the disposal of the international community that can be deployed to enhance the prospects of sustaining the peace. These include the introduction of peacekeeping forces, modest levels of investment in economic development and reconstruction, and supporting the establishment of a set of democratic political institutions that are tailored appropriately for the particular configuration of ethnic and religious cleavages in the society. One critical finding from several recent studies is that the longer the peace lasts, the less likely it is to break down into renewed conflict, regardless of the characteristics of the society, its economy, or its political system. Therefore, the critical task is to bring the conflict to an end and take the steps necessary to sustain it past the first few years, after which the peace becomes increasingly self-sustaining.

This analysis will not only review the evidence on what factors account for the duration of the peace (or, conversely, the prospects for renewed war), it will also offer theoretically grounded explanations of why we would expect each factor to have the effect that it does have on the durability of peace following civil war. These propositions will be illustrated with examples from specific cases. The analysis will conclude with a discussion of policy implications: what can be done to bring civil wars to an earlier and less destructive conclusion and prevent them from recurring, and how cost effective these policy interventions are compared to the cost of continued or renewed conflict.

SUSTAINING THE PEACE AFTER CIVIL WAR

It is widely recognized that over the last half century, civil war — revolution, secessionist conflict, and ethno-religious conflict — has replaced interstate war as the most frequent and deadly form of armed conflict in the international system. The Correlates of War (COW) Project, the long-standing armed conflict data archive project, reports that there were only 23 interstate wars between 1945 and 1997, resulting in 3.3 million battle deaths. By contrast, there were more than four times as many civil wars (108), resulting in almost four times as many casualties (11.4 million).[1] While COW includes only major armed conflicts, the Armed Conflict Dataset (ACD) compiled by the International Peace Research Institute of Oslo (PRIO) and Uppsala University codes major, minor and intermediate conflicts.[2] Of the 231 incidents identified in ACD as occurring between 1946 and 2005, 167 were internal conflicts, 21 were "extrastate" conflicts (mostly anticolonial wars), and only 43 were interstate wars.[3]

To date, the end of the Cold War has not brought much relief from the epidemic of civil wars. Harbom, Högbladh and Wallensteen report that since 1989 there have been 121 conflicts in 81 locations. Only seven of those conflicts were interstate wars; the rest were civil wars.[4] What the end of the Cold War did bring was the diffusion of civil war to Yugoslavia and the republics of the former Soviet Union. Following the dissolution of the Soviet Union into its constituent republics, civil wars erupted in the former Soviet republics of Georgia, Azerbaijan, Moldova, Tajikistan, and Russia itself. At the same time, the relatively peaceful secession of Slovenia from Yugoslavia was followed by secessionist revolts in Croatia and Bosnia. Eventually, Yugoslavia also dissolved into its constituent republics, with armed conflict continuing in Bosnia, Croatia, and Serbia-Kosovo. During the Cold War, these two nations and Europe generally had been more or less immune to armed rebellion on the scale of civil war. It is clear from these observations that, whether we are considering the Cold War era or its aftermath, *armed conflict since 1945 has been largely a matter of civil war.*

What is less often recognized about this same period is that once a nation experienced one civil war, it was highly likely to experience another one. The 108 civil wars in the COW data set occurred in only 54 nations. Only 26 of those nations experienced one and only one civil war, 10 had two civil wars, 12 had three, four had four, and two experienced five civil wars. The 124 civil wars listed in the Doyle and Sambanis data set occurred in just 69 nations. Only 36 of those nations had one and only one civil war, while 18 had two separate conflicts, nine nations had three, five nations had four, and one nation had five.[5] In an updated data set, Sambanis reports 151 civil wars occurring in 75 nations, with only 36 of those nations experiencing one and only one civil war, 20 nations had two, nine nations had three, four nations had four, five nations had five, and one nation (Indonesia) had seven civil wars.[6] This leads us to a second conclusion about patterns of armed conflict since 1945: *for a certain subset of nations, civil war has become a chronic condition.*

That observation raises the question of why it is so difficult to sustain the peace after a civil war. More precisely, what factors influence whether the peace established once a civil war ends will endure or, alternatively, the nation will experience a relapse into renewed civil war? These questions guide the analysis that follows. We begin with the proposition that the durability of the peace after a civil war is conditioned, first, by how the civil war ended: in a rebel victory, a government victory, or a negotiated settlement. This implies that to understand the durability of the peace following civil war — or, alternatively, the likelihood of peace failure and a resumption of civil war — we must first understand what factors determine whether the civil war ends in a rebel victory, a government victory, or a negotiated settlement.

A body of social science research has identified a set of national attributes that determine a nation's susceptibility to the initial outbreak of civil war. Presumably, these same factors should be implicated in the failure of peace (i.e., the relapse into renewed civil conflict) following the termination of a civil war. However, characteristics of the previous civil war itself — including its destructiveness, its duration, and the stakes of the conflict (e.g., secession versus revolution, ethnic versus ideological) — influence how the civil war will end. Independent of the national attributes that rendered the nation susceptible to civil war in the first place, characteristics of the civil war itself influence the cost-benefit calculations of the protagonists over the joint decision to continue fighting or stop. Combining the national attributes that define the risk set of nations that are susceptible to civil war with the conflict characteristics that predict how the civil war will end, we can identify a set of factors that condition the post-civil war environment in ways that make a relapse into civil war more or less likely or, alternatively, affect the capacity of the post-civil war regime to sustain the peace.

The question of how civil wars end points us to a third, more encouraging trend in the patterns of conflict since the end of the Cold War: the number of conflicts ongoing in any given year experienced a decline after 1992. Fearon and Laitin report that the annual number of ongoing conflicts rose steadily during the Cold War and peaked in 1994, declining thereafter.[7] Gleditsch *et al.*, using the more inclusive ADC, report a similar trend, with the number of conflicts peaking at 55 in 1992 and declining until 1996, after which the number has fluctuated between 30 and 35 ongoing conflicts in a given year.[8] Harbom *et al.*, report that this trend has held through 2005, when 31 conflicts were ongoing in the world.[9]

The decline in the number of ongoing conflicts in a given year is largely a function of a post-Cold War increase in the frequency with which ongoing conflicts have been brought to an end. It is not a function of any significant decline in the average number of new civil wars started per year. Fearon and Laitin report that the average annual rate of new civil war onsets (about 2.31) has remained rather constant for much of the last half century. What accounts for the steady increase in the number of ongoing conflicts during the Cold War is that the rate of new conflict onset exceeded the average annual rate at which conflicts ended (1.85), at least until about 1992.[10] The result was a relentless accumulation of ongoing conflicts. The number of ongoing conflicts declined after 1992 as a function of civil wars coming to an end at a faster rate than new civil wars have begun. And this trend is largely a function of the international community (primarily through the United Nations [UN]) assuming a more active role in brokering peace agreements to end protracted civil wars.

There was a brief surge in the number of new conflict outbreaks in the early 1990s, largely as a function of the breakup of the Soviet Union and Yugoslavia. Thus, more new wars started than ended in the first 5 years of the 1990s. This trend fueled public perceptions that the post-Cold War era would be fraught with danger. However, thereafter, the trend reversed: a greater number of wars ended than began during the latter half of the 1990s. The trend has continued into the new millennium: between 2000 and 2005 the number of conflicts that ended exceeded the number of new conflicts that began in each year, resulting in an average net decline of 1.5 conflicts per year.[11] The net effect is that by 2003 there were 40 percent fewer state-based conflicts underway than in 1992. Moreover, the number of high intensity conflicts (1000+ battle deaths) declined by 80 percent between 1990 and 2000.[12]

The increase in the number of civil war terminations over the last 15 years has been largely a function of an increase in the frequency with which civil wars have been brought to an end by negotiated settlements. Since the end of the Cold War more wars have been brought to a conclusion by negotiated settlement (42) than by military victory (23). By contrast, during the Cold War, the number of civil wars ending in military victory (by the government or the rebels) was twice as large as the number that were concluded by negotiated settlements. Hartzell reports that three-fourths of all conflicts that ended after 1990 did so by means of a negotiated settlement, whereas a majority of those that ended between 1950 and 1990 did so by means of a military victory by the government or the rebels.[13] Harbom *et al.*, report that one-third of the 121 conflicts that were active since the end of the Cold War (1989) have been brought to a conclusion by a formal peace agreement between rebels and government, a rate that is twice that for the previous 4 decades.[14] The trend accelerated in the new millennium: between 2000 and

2005, 17 conflicts ended in a negotiated settlement, while only four ended in military victory by the government or the rebels. In short, since 1990 negotiated settlement has surpassed military victory as the modal outcome in civil wars. Hartzell also points out that negotiated settlements reduce the human costs of civil war by ending them sooner. Military victories produced an average of 170,706 battle deaths whereas negotiated settlements produced only about half that number of deaths (87,487) and negotiated truces produced less than one-quarter of the death toll (35,182).[15] These observations lead to a third conclusion concerning patterns of conflict over the last half century: *since the end of the Cold War, more civil wars have been brought to an end by negotiated settlement than by military victory on the part of the government or the rebels.*

The debate over how civil wars end — and what the international community can do to bring them to an earlier and less destructive conclusion — has centered around two competing propositions. On the one hand, several studies note that the decline in the number of ongoing civil wars is largely a function of existing conflicts being brought to an end by third party mediation of negotiated settlements to protracted conflicts. The implication of this school of thought is that the best way to reduce the number of conflicts going on in the world is to build on this trend of international mediation to bring civil wars to an earlier and less destructive conclusion.

On the other hand, another group of scholars argues that, while brokering settlements to ongoing conflicts may bring them to a conclusion for now, peace agreements all too often preserve the protagonists' organizational capacity intact and thereby preserve the conditions for a resumption of conflict at a later date. Luttwak's "give war a chance" thesis contends that international mediation of civil wars "does little more than provide breathing space for warring parties to prepare for the next round of fighting."[16] As such, it simply makes recurrence of civil war more likely. Instead, Luttwak contends that it is preferable to "give war a chance": let the warring parties fight it out to a decisive military victory by one side or the other because the decisive defeat of one side makes it less likely that civil war will resume in that nation for some time. In other words, letting them fight it out until one side achieves decisive victory produces a more durable peace than brokering a peace agreement between the warring parties.

Explaining how civil wars end and what factors predict their recurrence is critical to any effort to devise policy remedies to reduce the frequency and destructiveness of armed conflict. The general patterns of conflict make this apparent. First, there is a set of national attributes that distinguish those nations that are at risk of civil war from those that are not. Second, nations that experience one civil war are highly likely to experience a relapse into armed conflict after the initial conflict has ended. Therefore, any policy prescriptions designed to reduce the amount of armed conflict in the international community should first target those nations that have experienced one civil war with policy interventions designed to minimize the risk of civil war recurrence. In order to design such interventions, we first must determine what factors affect the likelihood of a nation that has had one civil war relapsing into renewed conflict at a later date. Research suggests that the probability of civil war recurrence is influenced by (1) the attributes of the nation that put it at risk of civil war onset in the first place, (2) the manner in which the previous civil war ended — whether in a government victory, a rebel victory, or a negotiated settlement, (3) the attributes of the now-ended civil war that condition the post-conflict environment in ways that make the recurrence of civil war more or less likely, and (4) attributes of the post-conflict environment itself.

Drawing on recent empirical research on civil wars and the larger body of theoretical works on what factors make nations susceptible to civil war, I will present an analytical framework to assess these competing remedies for bringing civil wars to a conclusion and preventing them from recurring. I then use this framework to analyze recent findings on what factors predict how civil wars end and how long they last. This same framework provides us with some insights into what factors influence whether the peace will endure following the termination of a civil war or, alternatively, the peace will fail with a relapse into renewed conflict. These insights point to some policy prescriptions for sustaining the peace in the aftermath of civil war. I will conclude with a post-script on what this body of research suggests about how to end the war in Iraq.

DEFINING THE RISK SET: WHICH NATIONS ARE SUSCEPTIBLE TO CIVIL WAR?

Research on civil war onset has identified a set of national attributes that render a nation more or less susceptible to the outbreak of civil war. In effect they define the risk set of nations susceptible to the outbreak of civil war by specifying what national attributes distinguish those nations from the large majority of nations that are generally immune to civil war. Among the attributes that define this risk set are (1) the level of economic development, (2) the type of political regime (democracy, autocracy, or weak authoritarian), and (3) the degree of ethnic and religious fractionalization. It is reasonable to expect those same factors to be implicated in the recurrence of civil war or the failure of the peace after a civil war has ended.

Economic Development: Poverty Breeds Conflict.

The most consistent and robust finding across empirical studies of civil war onset is that economic underdevelopment (measured as gross domestic product (GDP) per capita, infant mortality rate, or life expectancy) is a significant predictor of civil war onset. Among all nations, those that are the most impoverished are at the greatest risk of experiencing civil war in a given year. Conversely, relatively prosperous nations are largely immune to civil war. Fearon and Laitin, Sambanis, Collier and Hoeffler, and others have found this relationship to be robust regardless of which civil war data set one uses or what statistical estimation technique or model specification one employs.[17] Fearon and Laitin report that "$1,000 less in per capita income is associated with a 41 percent greater annual odds of civil war onset." According to them, the poorest 10 percent of nations have an 18 percent chance of civil war breaking out in a given year, while the wealthiest 10 percent of nations have only a 1 percent chance of experiencing civil war onset in a given year.[18]

This finding provides empirical support for grievance-based theories of civil war: where more people suffer from deeper levels of poverty, grievances are likely to be more widespread and more deeply felt, and it is in such environments that civil wars are most likely to occur.[19] However, Collier and Hoeffler interpret this effect as a function of the opportunity costs of participating in armed rebellion.[20] The lower the average income in a nation, the lower the recruiting costs will be for rebel organizations. Where income and education levels are low (especially among young males), the payoffs from joining a rebel movement exceed what one can expect to earn by devoting one's time to conventional legal economic activity. This relationship is exacerbated by rapid population growth that often characterizes low-income nations. Rapid population growth creates "youth bulges" which overwhelm the supply of legal jobs and provide an ever-expanding pool of potential recruits for aspiring rebel movements.[21]

While the statistical relationship between measures of poverty and the probability of civil war onset is robust, there is nothing very surprising about this finding. There is nothing counterintuitive about the notion that civil war is more likely to occur in the most impoverished nations of the world. Moreover, it is still the case that, even among poor nations, most nations in most years do not experience an outbreak of civil war; civil war is still a rare event, in space and time, even among the most impoverished nations of the world. Fearon and Laitin's study identifies 127 new civil war onsets in all nations for all years from 1945 through 1997.[22] Out of a total of 6,610 nation-years in which a new civil war could have started, in only 127 of those nation-years did a civil war actually start. Therefore, the more challenging task is to specify, among poor nations, what factors distinguish those that do experience civil wars from those that do not, and in those that do, what factors determine the timing of civil war onset.

Regime Type: Democracy vs. Autocracy vs. Anocracy.

Drawing on the seminal work of Theda Skocpol, state-centric theories of civil war narrow the civil war risk set by proposing that, among impoverished nations, those governed by certain regime types are more susceptible to civil war than those governed by other regime types.[23] The task then becomes how to specify the regime types or regime characteristics that make a nation (especially an impoverished nation) more or less likely to experience a civil war onset in a given year.

The consensus is that *weak states* are more prone to violent opposition, including civil war. There is less agreement on what attributes define a state as weak. Barry Buzan argues that, "weak states either do not have or have failed to create a domestic political and social consensus of sufficient strength to eliminate the large-scale use of force as a major and continuing element in the domestic political life of the nation."[24] The state is seen by one or more significant social groups as representing the interests of a particular ethnic group (as is the case with many multiethnic states) or a particular social sector (such as the agrarian elite in Latin America) or an economic or military elite (as was the case in Nicaragua of the Somoza era or the Philippines of the Marcos era). Those who are not members of the group favored by the state withhold their support from the state, either tacitly by neglecting to comply with state laws and regulations and evading taxes, or actively by organizing opposition movements to challenge the incumbent regime. Because the state perceives those alienated social groups as a threat, it responds by increasing its coercive capacity in order to defend itself against anticipated challenges to its authority. The threat of state repression further alienates marginalized groups and gives them incentives to organize for armed rebellion. This cycle escalates into what Brian Job has termed an "insecurity dilemma."[25]

Regimes that manifest this *weak state syndrome* have been labeled *neo-patrimonial regimes*,[26] *sultanistic regimes*,[27] or *protection racket states*.[28] The common feature of these regimes is that they typically are headed by a personalist dictator presiding over a state apparatus that is staffed not on the basis of competence and experience but on the basis of personal loyalty to the dictator.

Goodwin identifies five practices common to weak states that render them susceptible to armed revolt. This list captures most of the attributes that others have listed as characteristic of the weak state syndrome. First, *state sponsorship of unpopular social and economic arrangements* makes the state the target for the grievances that the extremes of poverty and economic inequality generate.[29] These arrangements can be based on class differences or ethnic differences. Stanley's protection racket state is typical of the former: in a nation such as El Salvador, where export agriculture was the dominant sector of the economy, the military protected the interests of a small landed elite from redistributive pressures emerging from the large landless and land-poor peasant population. The military systematically repressed dissent and dissident organizations among the peasants, thereby preserving the landed elites in control over landed wealth. In return, the military was allowed to control the institutional machinery of the state and use it to extract rents from society for the purposes of enriching the officer corps.[30] Where ethnic differences are the basis of the unpopular social and economic arrangements, a dominant ethnic group uses its control over the institutional machinery of the state to further subordinate other ethnic groups, economically, politically, and socially, through discriminatory laws and practices. The dominance of the Hutu majority in Rwanda under Juvenal Habyarimina or the Sinhalese majority in Sri Lanka is exemplary of this arrangement.[31]

Second, where a *weak state excludes newly mobilized groups from access to state power or economic opportunity*, it may leave those groups with few alternatives other than direct challenges to the state's authority.[32] The regime types listed earlier are, as a rule, intolerant of any sort of grassroots political mobilization. When collective dissent does emerge, such states typically react with repression. This leaves even moderate reformers with few options other than withdrawing from politics and suffering in silence or resorting to violent tactics of their own. Otherwise, those leaders risk being marginalized among their own constituents for being ineffectual. Even the choice of withdrawing from politics is not viable because, as known leaders of an opposition organization, they have to assume that they remain on the state's list of targets for repressive violence. Hence, they have powerful incentives — i.e., the threat of being victims of state-sanctioned repression — to remain active in opposition politics but to shift to violent tactics of their own.[33] Repression tends to radicalize dissent.

Third, when confronted with political opposition, weak states typically respond with *indiscriminate but not overwhelming repressive violence*, which tends to radicalize the opposition.[34] Mason and Krane argue that the escalation to indiscriminate violence is highly

13

likely among weak states, in part because they lack the institutional capacity or redistributable resources to pursue more accommodative reform strategies. Moreover, given the origins and composition of such regimes, they also generally lack the political will to pursue reform and accommodation as opposed to repression. Repression is the one policy response for which weak states are well-equipped. Therefore, when confronted with opposition challenges, they almost reflexively employ the resources with which they are best endowed: the repressive machinery of the state.[35]

Usually the state begins by targeting opposition leaders. This compels those leaders who manage to escape the repressive arm of the state to go underground and shift to violent tactics of their own. Lacking sufficient numbers to mount insurgent attacks, the small surviving cadre of opposition leaders often resorts to forms of terrorist violence intended to provoke the state into expanding its repressive targeting, thereby driving more people to the side of the opposition. If the state's initial efforts to decapitate the opposition do not silence it, the weak state typically responds by expanding repression to include rank and file participants in and supporters of opposition organizations and social movements. They target members of labor unions, political parties, peasant associations, and other social organizations that have some degree of autonomy from the state, some established constituency, and a record of public opposition to the state, its leaders, and its policies. When repression becomes more widely targeted, nonelite supporters of opposition movements are then compelled to go underground as well. This provides the previously radicalized dissident leadership with the human resources to escalate terrorist violence to guerrilla insurgency. Faced with the escalation of opposition violence, weak states typically respond by further expanding the targeting of their repression to include the civilian support base of the insurgent opposition.[36]

At this point, distinguishing the guerrilla irregular and his/her supporters from the uninvolved civilian presents the state's security forces with the classic *counterinsurgency dilemma*.[37] Troops in the field, whose immediate goal is to survive the mission, are likely to target anyone remotely suspected of supporting the insurgents rather than risk allowing a suspected insurgent to escape detection and later kill them. As Leites and Wolf put it, without adequate intelligence to allow them to target rebel supporters and only rebel supporters, government security forces "may not feel too guilty about fulfilling their professional duty of spending ammunition."[38] From the point of view of civilians, the indiscriminate application of state repression means that their chances of being victimized are largely unrelated to whether or not they actually support the insurgents, actively or tacitly, overtly or covertly. Under those circumstances, it may become rational for them to join the insurgents if for no other reason than to secure protection from indiscriminate counterinsurgent violence by the state's security forces.[39]

In this sense, repression by itself can and often does fail to suppress opposition. Instead, it can instigate the escalation from nonviolent protest to violent opposition and, eventually, civil war. It may bring about a temporary lull in opposition activity in the early stages, largely by disrupting the ability of conventional (nonviolent) opposition organizations to mobilize their supporters. However, once a campaign of repression begins, it is difficult to keep it from becoming indiscriminate. Over the longer term, as repression escalates, it is likely to become indiscriminate, which compels opposition organizations to shift to violent tactics of their own and, eventually, to escalate the level of violence from terrorist acts to low level insurgency to civil war.

Fourth, Goodwin points to *weak policing practices and infrastructural power* that enable insurgent groups to establish security zones within the territorial jurisdiction of the state.[40] From secure base areas, insurgents can mount and sustain armed challenges to the state. There are two components of this dimension of state weakness. First, if the state's policing power is geographically uneven, then rebels can establish secure bases of operation in those regions where the state's police presence is weakest. Fearon and Laitin found evidence that geographic features of a nation that make it easier for insurgents to establish secure base camps increase that nation's susceptibility to civil war.[41] The second component is a function of the state's relationship with the population. Where large segments of the population are alienated from the state, the state's power becomes more strictly a function of its troop strength. It cannot count on the population to provide it with intelligence on rebel operations. Indeed, all that insurgents need in order to survive is a population that tolerates their existence, which amounts to a form of tacit support. Leites and Wolf observe that, "the only 'act' that [the rebel] needs desperately from a large proportion of the populace is nondenunciation (that is, eschewing the act of informing against R[ebels]) and noncombat against [them]."[42] Joel Migdal adds, "in the early stages of revolution, revolutionaries stake their lives on the hope that peasants will not expose them to authorities."[43]

Neo-patrimonial regimes are especially prone to weak policing capability because their security forces, like other state institutions, are staffed according to their loyalty to the leader, not their competence. As long as the security forces remain loyal, the leader is usually tolerant of a certain level of corruption, incompetence and venality on their part. This simply exacerbates the state's weakness by alienating the civilian population as a source of intelligence on the rebels and driving them to the side of the rebels.

Finally, Goodwin argues that the corrupt and arbitrary rule of neopatrimonial dictators tends to *alienate, weaken, and divide elite groups and external supporters* who otherwise might share the leader's interest in repressing opposition challenges.[44] For this reason, neopatrimonial regimes are not only susceptible to revolutionary challenges but also vulnerable to defeat by them. When an opposition challenge escalates to the point of posing a threat to the survival of the state, whatever elite coalition has supported the regime can quickly dissolve if elements of that coalition become dissatisfied with the dictator's distribution of the spoils of rule among his coalition of supporters. Signs of divisions within the elite coalition are often readily apparent, and insurgents can exploit them by escalating the level of violence. A military establishment that has been deprofessionalized by the corruption that is tolerated by the neopatrimonial leader as the price for the military's loyalty can quickly dissolve in the face of an effective rebel challenge, especially when they see the leader's civilian coalition defecting and his ability to deliver the spoils of patronage eroding. The sudden collapse of the Somoza regime in Nicaragua, the Mobutu regime in Zaire, and the Barre regime in Somalia illustrate the vulnerability of neopatrimonial regimes not only to the emergence of armed challenges but to defeat by them.

The empirical evidence on the susceptibility of weak states to civil war is generally supportive, though hampered by measurement issues. Fearon and Laitin argue that "financially, organizationally, and politically weak central governments render insurgency more feasible and attractive due to weak local policing and corrupt counterinsurgency practices."[45] However, their statistical models include no direct measure of these aspects of the weak state syndrome. They add that weak states have "a propensity for brutal and indiscriminate retaliation that helps drive noncombatants into rebel forces," an argument that echoes Mason and Krane's theory about the impact of escalating repression on the distribution of popular support between the state and the opposition. However, Fearon and Laitin's models contain no direct measure of this weak state characteristic either. Indeed, their primary measure of state weakness is income per capita, which most theories of civil war onset treat as a measure of grievances[46] or opportunity costs,[47] not state strength.

The more common test of the relationship between state strength and civil war is the *domestic version of the democratic peace proposition*: that democracies are less susceptible to civil war than are nondemocracies. Numerous studies have tested this proposition, employing the 21-point (+10 to -10) POLITY IV democracy-autocracy scale. States with scores of 7 or more on this scale are treated as full democracies, while those with scores of -7 or below are treated as fully autocratic regimes. Both fully democratic and fully autocratic states are treated as "strong" states, at least in the sense of their capacity to avoid civil war. It is the middle range of "weak authoritarian regimes"

(-6 to 0), "semi-democracies" (0 to +6), or (generally) "anocracies" (-6 to +6) that are alleged to be the most prone to civil war.

At one end of the scale, democracies are less likely to experience civil war because civil war is not necessary for the opposition to have its concerns accommodated (or at least considered) by the state.[48] Under democracy, opposition groups are free to organize for peaceful collective action, to form their own political parties and run candidates for office, and otherwise to engage in a variety of forms of peaceful collective action to seek redress of grievances or to secure the enactment of their preferences into policy. And they are free to do so without fear of state repression. Elections confront political leaders with incentives to accommodate popular demands in order to expand their vote share. Those same electoral incentives discourage state leaders from employing repression against a loyal opposition, lest those leaders suffer the repercussions at the polls.

At the other end of the scale, fully autocratic regimes are also unlikely to experience civil war because they possess the overwhelming coercive capacity to repress opposition movements preemptively. In autocracies, rebellion is irrational because the coercive capacity of the state is so overwhelming that dissident movements are crushed before they can mobilize any base of popular support. Citizens are intimidated into withholding support for or participating in such movements for fear of the severe repressive consequences.[49]

It is that middle range of weakly authoritarian regimes or semi-democracies that are most prone to civil war because they lack the institutional capacity to accommodate peaceful opposition movements or the coercive capacity to repress them preemptively. The findings on the democracy/autocracy-civil war relationship are mixed, but generally, there is support for this "inverted-U" relationship: fully democratic regimes and highly autocratic regimes are less likely to experience civil war, while weak authoritarian regimes and semi-democracies are most susceptible to civil war.[50]

A critical addition to this hypothesis is the finding by Hegre *et al.*, that new democracies—i.e., regimes that have recently undergone the transition to democracy—are especially susceptible to civil war. Indeed, *change in a nation's level of democracy*—regardless of whether it is becoming more democratic or more autocratic—appears to be especially destabilizing.[51] New democracies may have the formal institutions to accommodate dissident interests in a peaceful manner, but it takes time for a civic culture to emerge whereby the population views democratic processes as "the only game in town." Until a stable party system evolves, elections create space for anti-democratic demagogues to run for office and win. Unchecked by an effective and institutionalized "loyal opposition," such leaders can use the power of elective office to attack rival leaders and their parties and gradually but inexorably transform a fledgling democracy into what Fareed Zakaria has termed an "illiberal democracy" that succumbs to the perverse principle of "one man, one vote, one time."[52] Such regimes are susceptible to civil war, despite the democratic facade that elections confer upon them. In Zimbabwe, once Robert Mugabe won that nation's first presidential election, he attempted to enact legislation to make Zimbabwe a one party state. When that failed (due to constitutional constraints established by the Lancaster House Agreement that ended the civil war), he accused his chief rival, Joshua Nkomo, of plotting an insurrection and unleashed a campaign of repression against Nkomo, his party, and his ethnic Ndebele support base. Zimbabwe has since degenerated into a virtual dictatorship that maintains only the thinnest veneers of democratic appearances. The empirical research discussed so far would suggest that Mugabe's rule has put Zimbabwe firmly in the risk set of nations susceptible to civil war.

Ethnic Divisions.

Among impoverished nations, those in which the population is fragmented along ethnic lines are especially susceptible to civil war. Indeed, ethnic fragmentation contributes to state weakness as well. In ethnically divided societies, the state itself can become the spoils over which ethnic groups compete. The state often does not command the support and loyalty of one or more ethnic groups. This is especially true where the state becomes dominated by one ethnic group to the exclusion of others. Excluded ethnic groups come to view the state as predatory, unresponsive to their interests at best and threatening to their ethnic identity at worst. Under these circumstances, the state comes to see itself as threatened by the excluded groups. As a result, a domestic security dilemma can emerge, whereby the state and excluded ethnic groups arm in order to defend themselves against the other, and each interprets the other's actions as a threat that warrants further arming.[53]

Shared ethnic identity serves as a powerful basis for mobilizing supporters for collective action. Dissident leaders can frame grievances in ethnic terms. Shared ethnic identity also facilitates recruitment by insurgent organizations. Dissident leaders can target their recruitment more efficiently to the extent that ethnic cleavages define the grievances that motivate rebellion. Shared ethnic identity also facilitates the identification and sanctioning of free riders in that defectors from a rebel movement can be identified by ethnic markers and sanctioned for not supporting the movement.

The findings on the relationship between ethnic fragmentation and the onset of civil war are surprisingly mixed. Most studies employ a version of the Ethnolinguistic Fractionalization Index (ELF) which uses the number and relative size of each ethnic group in a nation to calculate an index that estimates the probability that two randomly chosen individuals would be from different ethnic groups.[54] Theoretical arguments for the impact of ethnic fractionalization usually propose an "inverted-U" relationship between ELF and the likelihood of conflict: conflict is least likely in ethnically homogeneous societies and in those that are fragmented among a relatively large number of small ethnic groups, while ethnically based conflict is most likely in societies that are divided between a small number of relatively large ethnic groups.

Where society is composed of a large number of relatively small ethnic groups, no single group has sufficient numbers to threaten the establishment of ethnic hegemony over the other groups. Ethnic security dilemmas that would motivate groups to mobilize and arm defensively—and thereby motivate a similar response on the part of other ethnic groups—are less likely to arise because no single ethnic group is large enough to pose a threat of ethnic dominance. Collier and Hoeffler add that in highly fragmented societies, coordination problems between ethnic groups reduce the likelihood that multiple ethnic groups will be able to form a coalition of sufficient magnitude to mount and sustain a major rebellion.[55] Each group has little incentive to devote much of its collective resources to political activities beyond its own communal borders.[56] The state is more able to accommodate the demands of one group without threatening the interests of the others.

By contrast, where there are fewer groups and one or more is sufficiently large in number (relatively and absolutely) to aspire to ethnic hegemony, ethnic security dilemmas are more likely to arise, making conflict more likely.[57] If one group mobilizes to assert its control over the machinery of the state, other groups are likely to react defensively by mobilizing and perhaps arming themselves to prevent that or to defend their group against subordination by the group aspiring to dominance.

Elbadawi and Sambanis did find support for an inverted-U relationship between the degree of ethnic fractionalization and the probability of civil war.[58] Elbadawi and Reynol-Querol found that ethnically polarized societies (i.e., those divided between two ethnic groups) have a greater risk of experiencing civil war.[59] Similarly, Collier and Hoeffler did find a relationship between civil war onset and a condition of "ethnic dominance," defined as a nation in which the largest ethnic group constitutes between 45 and 90 percent of the population.[60] Ellingsen also found that societies that were divided among a relatively small number of relatively large groups were more likely to experience civil war.[61] Her key measure was the relative size of the *second* largest ethnic group. Cederman and Girardin found that governments controlled by ethnic minorities are more likely to experience civil war, and the smaller the ratio of the dominant ethnic group's size to a challenger group's size, the more likely civil conflict is to arise between those two groups.[62]

However, neither Fearon and Laitin nor Collier and Hoeffler found much support for a direct relationship between the degree of ethnic fractionalization and the probability of civil war.[63]

These findings suggest that ethnic civil war is more a function of the ability of groups to mobilize for violent collective action than of the depth of the ethnic grievances that motivate rebellion.[64] The extent to which an ethnic group is concentrated geographically strongly affects its ability to mobilize.[65] Ethnic minorities that are concentrated in their own territorial enclave are less subject to monitoring and repression by rival ethnic groups than are groups that are interspersed among other ethnic groups (including a dominant ethnic group). Geographic concentration also makes it easier for the group to establish secure base camps from which to organize and sustain an armed rebellion. Geographic concentration also facilitates the detection and sanctioning of free riders among the members of the group.[66]

Resource Wars: Do Oil, Drugs, and Gems Fuel Conflict?

A recent addition to the civil war research program has been the *resource curse* hypothesis: nations that are heavily dependent on mineral exports as a source of national income are especially susceptible to civil war. There are two streams of research that come out of this program. The first is that oil-exporting nations are prone to state weakness and, therefore, civil war. Oil wealth increases the value of controlling the state and, as such, creates incentives for rebel groups to emerge and challenge the incumbent government for control of the state.[67] Similarly, oil wealth creates incentives for regional ethnic groups to launch secessionist wars intended to wrest control of oil-rich regions from the existing regime.[68]

The second theme in this literature is the "greed" hypothesis, championed by Paul Collier and his colleagues at the World Bank. They propose that civil war is driven not so much by grievance as by greed. That is, civil war is more likely where rebel organizations have access to "lootable" commodities, such as illegal drugs or gemstones. What makes these commodities valuable for rebels is that they can be produced only in limited geographic regions. Only some nations have deposits of gemstones, and those deposits are located in very specific regions of those countries. Illegal drugs such as opium and coca can only be grown in certain climates, altitudes, and soil types. Where rebels can capture the territory where such commodities are produced or control the supply routes from production sites to markets, they can extract rents from this sector of the economy that they can use to finance their rebellion.

In Peru, Shining Path guerrillas provided coca growers with protection from drug eradication efforts of the government. They also provided protection for a number of clandestine landing strips in remote regions of the Andean highlands where drug cartels could fly in planes to transport coca leaf or coca paste to laboratories outside the country. Protection fees from coca growers and landing fees from drug cartels produced a revenue stream that enabled the rebel organization to equip and pay guerrilla soldiers.[69] Revolutionary Armed Forces of Colombia (FARC) guerrillas have developed a similar symbiotic relationship with coca growers there, as has the Taliban (and, before them, regional warlords) with opium poppy growers in Afghanistan.

Rebels in Congo/Zaire, Sierra Leone, and Angola have sustained their operations with revenues from alluvial diamonds.

Empirical support for the "greed" hypothesis is somewhat mixed. A stronger case can be made for lootable resources contributing to the duration of civil war rather than to the onset of civil war.[70] Fearon finds that the availability of lootable resources is positively associated with the duration of civil wars, especially secessionist conflicts in peripheral regions of a nation where the resources are located.[71]

A related element of the "resource curse" thesis is that oil exporting nations are particularly susceptible to civil war, especially of the secessionist variety. The logic underlying this relationship is that the rents that can be derived from oil exports create incentives for rebel groups to contest over control of the state or for regional groups to seek secession in the hopes of gaining monopoly control over oil-rich regions in a country.[72] Ross adds that the same incentives can induce external intervention in civil wars, as was the case with Liberian President Charles Taylor's intervention into the conflict in Sierra Leone.[73] Fearon and Laitin argue that oil wealth contributes to state weakness, which in turn makes civil war more likely.[74] States that derive significant rents from oil revenues have the capacity to "buy" popular quiescence by providing extensive social welfare benefits, without investing in developing a growth economy that would be sustainable even without oil revenues. Humphreys adds that dependence on mineral exports can retard the growth of domestic commerce, thus making the nation more vulnerable to external shocks, such as rapid declines in the price of oil.[75] Leaders of oil-rich nations can also use the rents from oil exports to finance extensive the coercive machinery necessary to repress political opposition, a practice that (as discussed earlier) can have the effect of transforming nonviolent dissent into revolutionary opposition (especially where the payoffs from rebel victory—control over oil revenues—are so substantial).

Evidence on the "resource curse" explanation of civil war onset is mixed, with results highly dependent on how one measures natural resource dependence and how one specifies the dependent variable, civil war. Collier and Hoeffler find that a state's dependence on natural resource exports increases the likelihood that the nation will experience a civil war.[76] They do find that this effect is nonlinear: the probability of civil war increases up to a ratio of natural resource exports to GDP of 32 percent and declines beyond that point. However, Fearon and Laitin found no significant relationship (linear or otherwise) between primary commodity exports and civil war onset, though they did find that countries that derive at least a third of their export revenues from oil were twice as likely to experience civil war as similar nations that did not export oil.[77] Elbadawi and Sambanis found some support for this relationship but also found that such findings were highly sensitive to how the model was specified and which civil war data set one employed.[78] They concluded that the relationship is "fragile" at best and certainly not robust across data sets or model specifications. In a later paper, Collier and Hoeffler found that a nation's dependence on primary commodity exports is more strongly related to the onset of secessionist conflicts than revolutionary civil wars,[79] but Reynol-Querol presents evidence that revolutionary conflicts (rather than secessionist conflicts) are catalyzed by a dependence on primary commodity exports.[80] Part of the problem with this debate is that these studies lump together oil, and other minerals and even agricultural exports under the category of primary commodity exports, whereas the theories presented earlier focus separately on the effect of oil exports, on the one hand, and lootable commodities (such as illegal drugs or alluvial gemstones), on the other, on civil war onset.

The discussion up to now has surveyed the empirical findings and theoretical arguments on what national attributes define a risk set of nations susceptible to civil war. Impoverished nations with weak states define the broad parameters of this risk set. Among impoverished nations, those governed by neopatrimonial regimes appear to be especially vulnerable to civil war. Democracy does appear to immunize nations against civil war to some degree, but that effect emerges only after democratic institutions have been in place long enough to earn some degree of popular legitimacy and establish some degree of institutional stability. There is some evidence for a resource curse affecting the susceptibility of nations to civil war, but this effect is probably more catalytic than causal: oil-exporting nations that manifest the other risk factors may be somewhat more likely to experience civil war, but only if they manifest those other critical risk attributes such as state-weakness and widespread poverty. Ethnic divisions exacerbate most of these risk factors: weak states presiding over impoverished populations that are also ethnically divided are more likely to experience civil war than similar nations that are not divided among a small number of relatively large ethnic groups. Moreover, the pacifying effects of democracy are less likely to emerge—and democracy is less likely to survive—in ethnically divided societies.

With this survey of what makes nations susceptible to civil wars, we now turn to the question of how civil wars end and what factors influence the durability of the peace following the termination of civil war.

WIN, LOSE, OR DRAW: HOW CIVIL WARS END

While an extensive body of research has defined a set of national attributes that define the risk set of nations susceptible to civil war, there is considerably less research on how civil wars end or what factors predict the durability of the peace after civil war. This author has completed several studies on these subjects, and some findings appear to hold up across data sets and model specifications.

A useful way to think about how civil wars come to an end is to consider the decision calculus by which rebels and governments decide whether to stop fighting or continue to prosecute the war. The model I present is built on the assumption of two rational actors involved in a civil war. The rationality assumptions and the assumption of two decisionmakers are, admittedly, an over-simplification of the reality of civil war. However, models such as these are evaluated on the basis of whether they enable us to derive some predictions about what conditions affect how civil wars end and whether those predictions are supported by evidence from the real world. This decisionmaking model has been used to identify what conditions make a civil war more likely to end in a negotiated settlement rather than a military victory by either side, and the model correctly predicted 87 percent of the outcomes.[81] It has been used to predict whether a civil war will end in a government victory, a rebel victory, or a negotiated settlement, and it correctly predicted 86 percent of the outcomes in that study.[82] Most recently, it was used to predict whether a nation that had experienced one civil war would experience a relapse into renewed civil war, and that model correctly predicted recurrence/nonrecurrence 85 percent of the time.[83] It has also been used to model the duration of civil wars,[84] and the duration of the peace after a civil war.[85] Similar logic has also been used to explain how interstate wars end,[86] and how foreign intervention affects the duration of civil wars.[87] Thus, whatever one might think about the realism of rationality assumptions or the extent to which the decision calculus oversimplifies the reality of civil war, the model does allow us to develop some predictions about what factors affect civil war outcome, and those predictions are supported by the empirical evidence.

At any given point in a civil war, the government (G) and the rebels (R) each must choose between quitting or continuing to fight. This implies four possible outcomes from their joint decisions at any given time, t_i: (1) if R continues fighting and G quits, R wins and the government is overthrown; (2) if G continues to fight and R quits, G wins and the revolt is defeated; (3) if both G and R choose to quit at the same time, the civil war ends in a truce or a negotiated settlement; (4) if neither decides to quit, the civil war continues. Following Stam, the four outcomes can be represented as an iterated two-person game (see Figure 1), with continued fighting as the dominant strategy for both sides.[88] If one or both parties prefer to continue fighting, it must be that they expect either to win at some point in the future or at least achieve more favorable settlement terms than what they estimate they can secure in the present. In either case, as long as one or both parties expect that their net benefits from victory (or a future settlement) will exceed the benefits they can get from a settlement now (or from defeat), they have a strong incentive to continue fighting.

		GOVERNMENT	
		Fight	Quit
REBELS	Fight	Civil War Continues	Rebels Win
	Quit	Government Wins	Negotiated Settlement
Derived from Allan C. Stam III, *Win, Lose, or Draw: Domestic Politics and the Crucible of War*, Ann Arbor, University of Michigan Press, 1996, p. 35.			

Figure 1. Civil War Outcomes as a Function of Rebel and Government Choices.

The decision calculus by which both actors choose between continuing to fight and stopping is a function of the expected payoffs from victory versus defeat versus a negotiated settlement.[89] The expected payoffs from continuing to fight are a function of: (1) the actor's subjective estimate of the total payoffs from victory, (2) the actor's estimate of the probability of victory, (3) the actor's estimate of the rate at which s/he will have to absorb the costs of conflict if s/he continues to fight in hopes of eventually achieving victory, (4) the actor's estimate of the amount of additional time needed to achieve victory (and, therefore, the amount of time that actor will have to absorb the costs of conflict in order to achieve victory). Mason and Fett represent the expected utility of continuing to fight as follows:

$$EU_C = P_V(U_V) + (1 - P_V)(U_D) - \sum_{t_i=0}^{t_v} C_{ti} \qquad (1)$$

where EU_c is the expected utility of continuing to fight, U_v is the actor's estimate of the payoff from eventual victory, P_v is the actor's estimate of the probability of achieving victory, U_d is the actor's estimate of the cost from defeat, $(1-P_v)$ is the estimated probability of defeat, C_{ti} is the actor's estimate of the rate at which the costs of conflict will accrue from the present (t_0) to that time in the future when the actor estimates victory can be achieved (t_v). Generally, an actor will continue to fight as long as its expected payoff from victory $(P_v U_v)$ exceeds the costs it expects to absorb in order to achieve

victory $(\sum_{t_i=0}^{t_v} C_{ti})$. However, even if one protagonist believes its chances of victory are better than even, that actor may still prefer to seek a negotiated settlement if its estimate of the cumulative costs required to achieve victory come to approach or exceed its expected payoff from victory. Under these circumstances, victory, even though more likely than defeat, would be pyrrhic.

For a negotiated settlement to be preferred to continued fighting, the expected utility of a negotiated settlement, EU_s, must be greater than the expected utility of continuing the conflict, EU_c. The expected utility of a negotiated settlement can be represented as follows:

$$EU_s = P_s(U_s) + (\sum_{t_i=0}^{t_v} C_{ti}) - \sum_{t_i=0}^{t_s} C_{ti} \tag{2}$$

where U_s represents that actor's estimate of the payoffs from the terms of the settlement and the cost terms are the same as in Equation (1). The payoffs from a settlement (U_s) are presumed to be less than the payoffs from victory (U_v). However, by agreeing to a settlement now rather than continuing to fight in search of victory, the actor saves the additional costs of conflict that would have to be absorbed in order to achieve victory ($\sum_{t_i=0}^{t_v} C_{ti}$). Instead, that actor has to absorb only those additional costs that accrue between the present and that time in the more immediate future (t_s) when the settlement goes into effect and the fighting stops ($\sum_{t_i=0}^{t_s} C_{ti}$; we assume that $t_s < t_v$).

The logic of this decision calculus implies that any factor that (1) decreases an actor's estimate of the probability of victory (P_v), (2) reduces that actors's estimate of the payoff from victory (U_v), (3) increases the rate at which that actor absorbs the costs of continued conflict (C_{ti}), or (4) extends that actor's estimate of the time required to achieve victory (t_v) should make negotiating a settlement more attractive than continuing to fight. From this decision calculus, we can derive some propositions concerning the characteristics of a civil war that affect the outcome of the conflict by influencing one or both party's incentives to continue fighting, capitulate, or enter negotiations for a settlement.

Duration Matters.

The decision calculus implies, first, that the longer a civil war last, the more likely it is to end in a settlement (as opposed to a military victory by either side). Indeed, one fairly consistent finding on civil war outcomes is that *the longer a civil war lasts, the less likely it is to end in a decisive military victory by either the government or the rebels.* If the rebels win (the least likely outcome), they typically do so within the first few years of the conflict. Mason, Weingarten, and Fett found that 12 of 16 rebel victories in their data set of 57 civil war terminations (1945-92) occurred within the first 5 years of the conflict. Similarly, if governments succeed in putting down a rebellion decisively, they also usually do so within the first 5 years of the conflict. They also found that all but three of 28 government victories occurred within the first 5 years of the conflict.[90] If neither side prevails early, the conflict settles into a *mutually hurting stalemate* in which neither side has the capacity to defeat the other, but each side has sufficient strength to prevent their own defeat.[91] At that point, the only way out of the conflict is through a negotiated settlement. Otherwise, the conflict simply drags on interminably. Mason and Fett (1996) found that negotiated settlement was by far the most likely outcome to civil wars lasting more than 5 years.[92] Fearon found that one-quarter of the civil wars that occurred between 1945 and 1997 lasted 2 years or less, and another quarter lasted at least 12 years; 13 lasted 20 years or more.[93] Consistent with Mason, Weingarten, and Fett's study, he found that those that ended quickly terminated in a decisive victory by one side or the other while those of long duration ended in a negotiated settlement or simply dissipated after reaching a protracted stalemate. Fearon concludes *"civil wars last a long time when neither side can disarm the other, causing a military stalemate. They are relatively quick when conditions favor a decisive victory"* (emphasis in the original).[94]

These findings imply that, contrary to Edward Luttwak's "give war a chance" thesis, civil wars will not burn themselves out like brush fires, nor will the conditions of a more lasting peace emerge naturally from the course of the war if the international community simply stands aside and allows the protagonists to fight it out to a decisive victory by one side or the other. The decisive military victory that Luttwak claims will produce a more lasting peace occurs early in the conflict or it usually does not occur at all. Civil wars that do not end in early victory simply drag on, disrupting the nation's economy, destroying its infrastructure, and bleeding its population. Protracted civil wars may wax or wane in intensity, but they rarely burn themselves out. Contrary to Luttwak's recommendation, if the international community does choose to stand aside and "give war a chance," what will result is not a more durable peace but a protracted bloodletting that is not likely to end on its own and, even if it does, will leave the nation so decimated that it immediately becomes a prime candidate for a relapse into renewed civil war. Once protracted conflicts have settled into a mutually hurting stalemate, they are "ripe for resolution" (in Zartman's words). However, as I will discuss later, breaking the stalemate usually requires the involvement of a third party to serve as mediator. Left to their own devices, protagonists in a civil war are rarely able to get to a settlement on their own, for reasons that Barbara Walter has spelled out and which I will discuss later.[95]

The duration of the conflict affects the outcome in several ways. First, the progression of a civil war is an information revealing process, in the sense that the experience of ongoing conflict forces both the government and the rebels to revise their estimates of their chances of victory and the costs they will have to absorb to achieve victory. The longer the conflict lasts, the more likely both sides are to discount their estimate of their chances of achieving victory (P_v). Likewise, the experience of a protracted conflict compels them to adjust their estimate of the amount of time required to achieve victory (t_v) and, therefore, the cumulative costs required to achieve victory ($\sum_{t_i=0}^{t_v} C_{ti}$).

For conflicts ending in government victory, there is evidence that the size of the government's army as a proportion of the nation's population does increase the odds of government victory and shortens the time to government victory.[96] DeRouen and Sobek also found that increases in the relative size of the government's army shorten the war; however, they did not find that it affected which side won, only that the conflict ended sooner.[97] These findings on the effect of the government's military follow from the cost of conflict factor in the decision calculus presented earlier: where governments have a relatively large army, they can inflict heavy costs on the rebels early and thereby prevail. Rebels start out with a decided military disadvantage: they have to build a military force from scratch in the shadow of a government that already has an established military capability. Thus, we would expect rebels to be especially vulnerable to early defeat. Given this initial disadvantage, if rebels overestimate their chances of victory when they initiate the conflict, they are subject to an early and decisive defeat. The example of Ché Guevara in Bolivia illustrates this vulnerability. Guevara found little interest among Bolivian peasants in his call for armed uprising against landlords, the Bolivian state or their foreign benefactors, in large part because land was relatively abundant in Bolivia.[98] Unable to recruit a guerrilla army or build a civilian support base of any size, Guevara was soon tracked down and his small armed band annihilated by the Bolivian government before it could build a base of support sufficient to avoid early defeat.

How, then, do we explain early victories by rebels? Previous research has suggested that the type of regime that is most susceptible to civil war—and the type most likely to be overthrown by an armed rebellion—is the neopatrimonial dictatorship described earlier. This regime type is marked by the dominance of a single personalist dictator presiding over a government and a military staffed on the basis of their loyalty to the dictator rather than their competence, training, or battlefield capabilities. Such regimes tend to be corrupt to the point of being parasitic and administratively incompetent. When challenging neopatrimonial regimes, rebels often prevail early, despite their initial disadvantage, because the government is so corrupt, incompetent, repressive, and parasitic that large segments of the population are willing to abandon the regime at the first sign that the rebels can win. Moreover, the state's own military is often deprofessionalized by the ethos of patronage and corruption that characterizes recruitment and promotion. Not only are they not very competent on the battlefield, their loyalty to the state is contingent upon the continued patronage of the dictator. When faced with a battlefield challenge, these militaries often collapse, with units choosing to desert or defect to what they see as a rebel bandwagon rather than risk their lives to defend a leader whose loyalty to them is suspect at best. Thus, when faced with a rebel challenge, a neopatrimonial regime often implodes as a result of its own corruption rather than as a function of the rebels' military capacity or tactical brilliance. Laurent Kabila had led a rebel movement in Zaire for 30 years (indeed, Ché Guevara went to work with him in 1965 only to depart later that year, frustrated by Kabila's unwillingness to prosecute the insurgency more aggressively). When Kabila's forces finally overthrew the Mobutu regime in 1997, their success was clearly more a function of the implosion of Mobutu's regime than of any change in Kabila's strategy, tactics, or level of popular support. The collapse of the Somoza regime in Nicaragua and the Lon Nol regime in Cambodia present additional examples of this effect. Not surprisingly, all of these regimes collapsed soon after external sponsors withdrew their support.

Another effect that is somewhat surprising is that the more deadly the conflict is (measured in casualties as a proportion of the population), the longer the conflict lasts. The decision calculus presented earlier implies that the deadliness of the conflict should shorten its duration as one or both sides calculate that the higher the rate at which they absorb costs, the shorter the time until the accumulated costs of conflict begin to approach the expected payoffs of victory. However, Brandt *et al.* (2005), found that higher casualty rates are associated with longer wars.[99] They interpret this as a "sunk cost" effect: the more deadly the conflict is, the more likely both sides are to continue fighting, perhaps in hopes of avenging or justifying the losses they have suffered up to that point.

Military Intervention Prolongs Civil Wars.

Contrary to the notion that major powers can impose a peace by intervening militarily in civil wars, the consistent finding across empirical studies is that military intervention by outside powers *in support of one side or the other* usually prolongs the conflict.[100] While counterintuitive at first glance — why would an outside power commit troops and treasure to a foreign military venture if it did not believe that action would enable its favored side to score a decisive victory? — when one considers the question of "What's in it for the intervener?" this effect makes more sense.

Intervention in another nation's civil war involves a substantial risk to the intervener, often with the promise of little direct payoff to the intervening nation.[101] On the downside, intervention does impose direct costs on the intervener, in terms of troops and treasure expended in prosecuting the intervention. Moreover, interventions also carry opportunity costs for the intervening nation. Military forces committed to the intervention are military forces not available for other national security needs. Funds expended on financing the intervention are funds not available for other national priorities. Finally, interventions carry political risks for the decisionmakers who initiate them. Audience costs to leaders can take a number of forms, from the risks that elected leaders will face at the polls to the risk that authoritarian leaders face in the form of opposition from within their own authoritarian coalition.[102]

Given the costs and risks, nations are more likely to intervene when the potential costs to that nation (including the political costs to the nation's leader) of *not* intervening come to approach or exceed those of intervening. Under what circumstances would this condition arise? When that nation's favored side in the civil war (whether the government or the rebels) is on the verge of defeat, it then becomes more feasible for the external power to intervene in order to prevent that defeat. If, for instance, an external power depends on another nation for some vital natural resource such as oil, and the government of that nation is in imminent danger of being overthrown by a rebel movement, then the risks of intervening can quickly be more than offset by the now-near certain costs that will follow from the overthrow of the incumbent regime, saddling the external power with the much greater (and more certain) costs that accrue from loss of access to that vital natural resource. The Cuban intervention in Angola took place not for the purpose of enabling the government of Angola to deal a decisive blow to UNITA rebels and end that civil war but to prevent the government's overthrow by those rebels. Similarly, the Soviet intervention in Afghanistan and the U.S. intervention in Vietnam were motivated by the desire to prevent the imminent overthrow of a favored government. Interventions of this type prolong the war by preventing the imminent defeat of the intervener's favored side in the conflict. Rarely do external powers intervene when their favored side is on the verge of victory. Why would a leader assume the risks and the costs of intervention when his/her preferred outcome is already imminent?

Direct military intervention in the form of sending armed forces into the middle of another nation's civil war is, of course, rare. More common are indirect forms of intervention, such as supplying one side or the other with funds and military equipment. Such measures also tend to prolong civil wars in that they represent a subsidy to that side's capacity to sustain combat operations. External support is a critical determinant of the duration of civil wars because the protagonists in a civil war, unlike their counterparts in an interstate war, draw on the same population and the same economy to sustain their operations. In the absence of external subsidies (in the form of foreign military and economic assistance to one or both sides), civil wars might come to an earlier conclusion simply as a function of the protagonists exhausting the human and material resources available to sustain armed conflict. In terms of the decision calculus presented earlier, subsidies to a civil war protagonist increase the amount of cost that actor can absorb in the quest for victory and extend the amount of time that actor can sustain combat in the quest for victory. The evidence suggests, however, that these subsidies serve to ward off defeat rather than enhance the prospects of victory or shorten the time to victory.

The importance of these subsidies can be seen in how quickly a number of civil wars came to an end after the Cold War waned and the two superpowers no longer had any compelling reason to continue subsidizing their favored side in these conflicts. The civil war in El Salvador and the Contra War in Nicaragua both ended in negotiated settlements, in part because the United States and the Soviet Union no longer had compelling (and competing) strategic interests in subsidizing their favored sides in these conflicts. Likewise, civil wars in Mozambique, Namibia, and Angola all came to an end soon after external support for one or both sides ended. Moreover, once Cold War rivalries disappeared from UN Security Council (UNSC) deliberations, the ability of that body to achieve the consensus necessary to authorize UN mediation of these conflicts was enhanced considerably, with the result being a remarkable increase in the frequency (and the success) of UN mediation of ongoing civil wars. Many of these mediation efforts would not have been possible during the Cold War because either the Soviet Union or the United States (or both) had (competing) interests at stake in these civil wars and, therefore, would have vetoed any UNSC resolution that would have jeopardized the ability of their favored side to prevail in the conflict.

SUSTAINING THE PEACE AFTER CIVIL WAR

Once a civil war ends, that nation is confronted with the reality that it is at grave risk of experiencing a relapse into renewed conflict. As noted earlier, nations that experience one civil war are highly likely to experience another. Indeed, a nation that has experienced one civil war is more likely to experience another one than a nation that has never had a civil war is to experience its first, even among those that are in the risk set of nations especially susceptible to civil war onset. To use a medical analogy, a nation that has had one civil war is like a person who has had a heart attack. That person is more likely to have another heart attack than are others who share the same risk factors but have so far not had their first heart attack.

What do we know about the factors that predict the relapse into renewed civil war? More precisely, what factors predict the duration of the peace after a civil war and, conversely, what factors predict peace failure? Two general conditions affect the durability of the peace after a civil war. First, for the peace to fail, a new rebel group (or a reconstituted old one) must develop the organizational capacity to mount an armed challenge to the post-civil war regime. The emergence of such a challenger represents what Charles Tilly has termed a condition of *dual sovereignty*, defined as a condition marked by "the appearance of contenders or coalitions of contenders, advancing exclusive alternative claims to the control over the government . . .; commitment to those claims by a significant segment of the subject population . . .; the incapacity or unwillingness of the government or its agents to suppress the challenger coalition . . ."[103]

For Tilly, dual sovereignty makes civil war possible. Therefore, the extent to which the condition of dual sovereignty persists or reemerges in the post-conflict environment affects the likelihood that the peace will fail with a relapse into civil war. Thus, factors that affect the extent to which dual sovereignty persists or reemerges in the post-conflict environment should affect the durability of the peace after civil war.

While dual sovereignty makes civil war possible, whether or not renewed civil war does erupt (and, if so, when) is a function of whether or not dissident groups have the incentive to revolt rather than sustain the peace. This element of agency can be modeled as a function of the potential rebels' estimate of the costs and benefits of resuming conflict versus sustaining the peace. This decision calculus is similar to that specified earlier in Equation 1.

Presumably, dissidents would prefer a resumption of conflict only if they believe they can eventually win or at least extract more favorable settlement terms in the future by resuming the fight now. The decision calculus presented earlier (Equation 1) can also be used to represent an actor's expected payoffs from resuming conflict versus sustaining the peace.[104] The payoff from resuming conflict is depicted as follows:

$$EU_C = P_V(U_V) + (1-P_V)(U_D) - \sum_{t_i=0}^{t_v} C_{ti} \qquad (3)$$

where EU_C is the expected utility of resuming the conflict, U_v is the actor's estimate of the payoff from eventual victory, P_v is the actor's estimate of the probability of achieving victory, U_d is the actor's estimate of the cost from defeat, $(1-P_v)$ is the probability of defeat, C_{ti} is the actor's estimate of the rate at which the costs of conflict accrue from the present (t_0) to that time in the future when the actor expects to achieve victory (t_v). For a resumption of civil war to be preferred, the expected utility of resuming the war, EU_c, must be greater than the expected utility of sustaining the peace, EU_p. The payoffs from sustaining the peace are:

43

$$EU_P = U_{P+} \sum_{t_i=0}^{t_v} C_{ti} \qquad (4)$$

where EU_p is the expected utility from sustaining the peace and U_s is the payoff from the post-civil war status quo. The payoff from the status quo is augmented by avoiding the costs that would have to be absorbed

in order to achieve victory ($\sum_{t_i=0}^{t_v} C_{ti}$).

This model suggests that any attribute of the post-conflict environment that (a) decreases the actor's estimate of the probability of victory (P_v), (b) decreases the actor's estimate of the payoffs from victory (U_v), (c) increases their estimate of the rate at which the costs of conflict would have to be absorbed to achieve victory (C_{ti}), (d) increases the protagonists' estimate of the time required to achieve victory (t_v), or (e) increases their estimate of the payoffs from sustaining the peace (U_p) should increase the duration of the peace following a civil war by reducing the incentives for that actor to initiate a new rebellion. One critical difference between the initial onset and the recurrence of civil war is that the experience of the previous war enables potential protagonists in the post-civil war environment to estimate more realistically the likely duration, costs, and probability of victory of a new war, information they did not have prior to the onset of the original war.

In summary, we expect the peace following a civil war to be less durable if (1) the condition of dual sovereignty persists in the post-war environment, and (2) for at least one politically mobilized group, the expected utility of resuming armed conflict is greater than the expected utility of sustaining the peace.

How a Civil War Ends Affects Whether Another Will Occur.

If the persistence or emergence of a condition of dual sovereignty affects the durability of the peace following a civil war, then the manner in which the previous civil war ended — whether in a government victory, a rebel victory, or a negotiated settlement — should affect the duration of the peace. The extent to which the condition of dual sovereignty that fueled the initial conflict persists after the war varies according to whether the rebels won, the government won, or the protagonists negotiated a settlement to the conflict.

Edward Luttwak's "give war a chance" thesis argues that negotiated settlements produce the most unstable peace because peace agreements preserve intact the organizational capacity of both sets of protagonists. Luttwak's argument is, in effect, that negotiated settlements preserve the condition of dual sovereignty and thereby make a relapse into civil war more likely. Even prior to Luttwak's provocative article, this proposition was the prevailing wisdom in studies on how civil wars end. Roy Licklider argues that arranging a peace settlement in a civil war is fundamentally more difficult than mediating interstate conflicts:

> Ending international war is hard enough, but at least there the opponents will presumably eventually retreat to their own territories. . . . But in civil wars the members of the two sides must live side by side and work together in a common government to make the country work. . . . How do groups of people who have been killing one another with considerable enthusiasm and success come together to form a common government?[105]

Harrison Wagner points out that the willingness of both sides to consider a negotiated settlement implies that "neither combatant has been able to disarm its adversaries." Any peace agreement will enable all of the protagonists in the civil war to retain some semblance of their organizational identities after the war, even if the agreement does provide for the disarmament and demobilization of their military wings.[106] In effect, the settlement leaves the nation one step — i.e., rearming — away from the reemergence of the condition of dual sovereignty that would make renewed civil war possible. Licklider presents empirical support for this proposition: civil wars that end in decisive military victory by one side or the other are less likely to experience a resumption of armed conflict than are conflicts that ended in a negotiated settlement.[107] The collapse of two peace settlements in Angola illustrates the fragile nature of negotiated settlements to civil wars, especially when the settlement does not provide for disarming the rival armies or integrating them into a single force before elections are held to select the new post-conflict government. When UNITA did poorly in the 1992 founding elections called for in the Bicesse Accords, UNITA leader Jonas Savimbi simply rejected the election results and returned to armed conflict as a means to win through renewed violence what he could not win at the polls.[108]

While Luttwak, Licklider, Wagner, and others predict that the peace is more durable following decisive victory in civil wars, all military victories are not alike. To date, few published studies have explored whether civil wars are more likely to recur following government victories or rebel victories.[109] The same logic of dual sovereignty that informs the "give war a chance" argument that settlements produce less durable peace than military victories would also suggest that rebel victories should produce a more durable peace than government victories. The defeat of an armed rebellion often represents little more than a lull in the fighting. Rebels on the verge of defeat can avoid annihilation by accepting defeat (for now) and blending into the population until they can rebuild their organization and their civilian support base to the point that renewed conflict becomes feasible. When the political opportunity structure becomes favorable, a new or revived rebel organization can reignite armed conflict. Examples of changes in the political opportunity structure that could suddenly make the reinitiation of rebellion feasible would be the death of a political leader, divisions within the governing elite, sudden economic or international military crises, and the withdrawal of foreign support for the incumbent regime.[110] The fact that civil war broke out earlier in that nation is *prima facie* evidence that a civilian support base of sufficient magnitude to sustain the original rebellion already existed in the nation. The civil war itself—no matter how long its duration or how severe its level of violence—certainly did nothing to improve whatever conditions gave rise to the grievances that fueled support for the original conflict. Indeed, civil war makes those conditions worse and generates new grievances as well. We know that nations that experience civil war are, on average, far more impoverished than other nations to begin with. In the aftermath of a civil war, then, a victorious government presides over a post-conflict environment that has been rendered even more susceptible to civil war by the destructiveness of the just-ended conflict. Unless the victorious government undertakes a significant program of reforms designed to "win the hearts and minds" of the civilian population, the conditions that fueled support for the original insurgency will not diminish simply as a function of the government having prevailed (for now) on the battlefield. And a victorious government is not likely to undertake such reforms, in part because it lacks the institutional capacity and redistributable resources to do so and in part because the civil war itself damaged an already weak economy and, thereby, diminished the tax base from which the victorious government could extract the revenues necessary to finance such reforms. For these reasons, the one strategy that a victorious government can pursue in order to reduce the ability of the defeated rebels to resuscitate their capacity to initiate and sustain a new armed rebellion is to engage in a campaign of repression designed to annihilate the last vestiges of the rebel organization and its civilian support base. Yet this campaign of repression is unlikely to win the hearts and minds of a war weary population. It certainly does nothing to resolve the conditions that fed their grievances in the first place. More than likely, it will simply expand the latent support base for renewed rebellion in the future.

By contrast, rebel victories are usually more decisive in terms of eliminating the condition of dual sovereignty. Officials of a defeated government (including the military) do not normally have the option of blending into the population and biding their time until conditions become ripe for them to mount their own armed challenge to the government installed by the victorious rebels. They do not have the luxury of anonymity that would allow them to blend into the population. On average, it will be easier for supporters of the victorious rebels to identify former soldiers who have tried to go underground than it would be for supporters of a victorious government to identify former insurgents who attempt to go underground. The leaders of defeated governments typically are either driven into exile, killed, or imprisoned.

There is some empirical support for the effect of civil war outcome on the duration of the peace after civil war, although to date there is far less research on this proposition than on civil war onset and duration. Quinn, Mason, and Gurses did find that rebel victories are less likely than government victories to be followed by a relapse into civil war.[111] They also found that negotiated settlements supported by peacekeeping operations are less likely to breakdown into renewed civil war than are government victories, a finding that casts some doubt on the "give war a chance" thesis that negotiated settlements are the most unstable form of civil war termination.[112] Mason, Gurses, Brandt, and Quinn found that the peace following a rebel victory is rather fragile for the first 2 years, but if victorious rebels can avoid an early resumption of armed conflict, the peace is more likely to endure than is the peace that follows a government victory.[113] When the Sandinistas overthrew the Somoza regime in Nicaragua, they were confronted with the Contra war within a matter of a few years. By contrast, after Fidel Castro's rebels overthrew the Battista regime in Cuba, his regime has managed to avoid a resumption of armed rebellion for almost 50 years. That same study also found that the peace following government victory was no more stable than the peace following negotiated settlements (again, in contrast to the "give war a chance" thesis) and that the introduction of peacekeeping forces reduced the odds of peace failure following a negotiated settlement by more than 70 percent.

Getting to an Agreement: Mediators and Mediation.

Even when a civil war becomes "ripe for resolution" by settling into a mutually hurting stalemate, no peace agreement is likely unless a third party agrees to mediate a settlement. Several studies have shown that the protagonists in a civil war are more likely to agree to negotiate, more likely to reach an agreement, and more likely to abide by the terms of that agreement when there is a third party to serve as mediator and to enforce the terms of the agreement.[114] Rebels and governments are unlikely to reach an agreement on their own, no matter what the cost-benefit ratio of a settlement outcome versus continued fighting. This is so because of the prisoner's dilemma they find themselves in with respect to the joint decision to stop fighting and negotiate a peace agreement. While both sides may estimate that they would be better off agreeing to a peace settlement than continuing to fight, each also knows that both parties' best outcome would be to get their rival to agree to a settlement and then cheat on the agreement after their rival has disarmed.[115] Third parties can resolve this dilemma by providing security guarantees to both sides.

Mediation of civil wars involves "a process of conflict management where the disputants seek the assistance of, or accept an offer of help from, an individual, group, state or organization to settle their conflict or resolve their differences without resorting to physical violence or invoking the authority of the law."[116] A third party mediator can facilitate the settlement process by, first, resolving some of the information problems that impede negotiations and reduce protagonists' incentives even to agree to negotiate. Both sides in peace negotiations have an incentive to misrepresent their capabilities and their goals. Since both sides are also aware that they both have this incentive, they have little reason to make sincere commitments in the negotiation process. A credible third party mediator can resolve some of these information problems.

Mediators can facilitate conflict resolution by providing a neutral setting for the parties to meet. What is more important is that a mediator can induce both sides to make concessions and encourage other behaviors that are conducive to a cease-fire or settlement agreement. Through the promise of resources, the mediator can make a settlement agreement more attractive than continued fighting. In effect, a mediator can contribute to a more durable peace by subsidizing the settlement outcome (i.e., increase U_s), thereby making the payoffs from a negotiated settlement relatively more attractive than the expected payoffs from continuing to fight. Finally, the mediator can make a settlement agreement more attractive by providing guarantees to enforce the terms of the settlement and to prevent either side from cheating on the terms of the agreement.[117]

Power-Sharing in Settlement Agreements.

While the "give war a chance" thesis contends that negotiated settlements produce the least stable peace, not all negotiated settlements are equally likely to break down into renewed conflict. In particular, peace agreements that include power-sharing arrangements make a negotiated settlement more durable. Carolyn Hartzell and her colleagues have shown that the more dimensions of power-sharing that are included in a peace agreement—i.e., military power-sharing, political power-sharing, economic power-sharing, and territorial power-sharing—the more durable the peace will be following a negotiated settlement.[118] Power-sharing arrangements of all types involve the creation of veto points and veto players in the post-conflict order. Power-sharing institutions are designed to give both sets of protagonists sufficient presence and representation in key policymaking institutions that each side can prevent the other from monopolizing control over that institution and using it to achieve by cheating on the peace agreement what they could not achieve on the battlefield: the subordination (or annihilation) of their rival.

The positive effect of power-sharing arrangements on the duration of the peace makes sense if we consider power-sharing institutions as mechanisms to dismantle the condition of dual sovereignty that made the original civil war possible and that would otherwise make the relapse into renewed civil war more probable. Military power-sharing arrangements usually involve disarming and demobilizing forces on both sides and their reintegration into a single national army. The terms of military power-sharing usually involve some formula for guaranteeing that both rebels and government forces will each be guaranteed a minimum share of the total number of troops and of the officer corps in a new, integrated national army. This provides both sides with some assurance that their former rival will not be able to monopolize control of the new army and use it against their former enemies. Where military power-sharing arrangements are not included in the peace agreement or where the peace agreement allows government and rebels to preserve their own separate security forces, the relapse into civil war is more likely.

Political power sharing arrangements revolve around the questions of institutional design for the post-civil war state. In particular, they focus on issues of presidentialism versus parliamentarism and proportional or majoritarian electoral systems. Political power sharing also focuses on issues of the allocation of administrative and civil service positions in the post-civil war regime. As discussed later, there is considerable debate on what institutional configuration—presidential versus parliamentary, proportional representation versus plurality electoral systems—produces the most enduring peace. However, there does seem to be some preference for parliamentary government over presidentialism, largely because a parliamentary system divides and constrains executive power to a greater degree than presidential systems. Second, a survey of the literature suggests a preference for proportional representation electoral rules over the plurality or majoritarian variant, largely because proportional representation systems provide minority groups with greater chances of gaining some representation in the legislature.

The demand for economic power sharing arrangements in settlement agreements is usually motivated by the concern that if one side in the civil war gains disproportionate control over the nation's economic wealth after the war ends, they will be able to use those assets to finance rearming for the purpose of annihilating their now disarmed opponent. Even short of security concerns, protagonists in peace negotiations may fear that if their rival is able to gain monopoly control over key economic assets, that rival may be able to use those resources to subordinate their rival economically.[119] Accordingly, groups will seek economic power sharing arrangements that "have the state displace or place limits on market competition, directing the flow of resources through economic public policies and/or administrative allocations to assist economically disadvantaged groups."[120]

Territorial power sharing involves decentralizing state power to regional units through federal arrangements or other forms of regional autonomy. This form of power sharing is especially relevant to securing a peace agreement in civil wars marked by geographically concentrated ethnic groups. Hartzell argues that territorial power sharing can lessen security fears and thereby make a peace agreement more acceptable to one or more parties in the negotiations. First, territorial power sharing provides some assurance that one group will not be able to seize monopoly control over the institutions of the state and use those to subordinate other groups under its authority. Groups will retain some autonomy within their own territory, and that autonomy will be formalized through the creation of the institutions of regional government. Thus, "territorial autonomy can serve to restrict authority at the political center by shifting decisionmaking power to subunits of the state."[121]

Spoilers in the Peace Process.

Getting civil war protagonists to the negotiating table in the first place is a major hurdle on the path to bringing about a sustainable peace in protracted civil wars. Getting them to come to terms on an acceptable settlement agreement is an even more daunting task. This task—as well as the next step of successfully implementing the terms of the agreement—is further complicated by the fact that rarely are the two sides in a civil war unitary actors. Governments involved in civil wars include factions of hardliners and moderates, distinguished from each other on the basis of their willingness to negotiate with the rebels, their preferences over what terms would or would not be acceptable in a peace agreement, and the resources they command that can be deployed for the purpose of influencing the outcome of the negotiations. Likewise, rebel forces often consist of coalitions of several armed groups, each with its own somewhat autonomous organizational structure, often with its own separate military organization and usually with its own somewhat distinct civilian constituency. Cunningham notes that 90 of the 288 internal conflicts in the Uppsala-PRIO Armed Conflict Data involved two or more rebel combat organizations active at the same time. Some conflicts involved more than 10.[122]

Rebel factions vary with respect to what settlement terms they would be willing to accept and what resources they have at their disposal to influence the course of the peace process. Divisions among rebel factions are further exacerbated where they are reinforced by ethnic divisions. Even if a mediator can get most of the factions on each side to agree to a settlement, extremist factions on either side (i.e., hardliners in the government or radicals among the rebels) who do not accept the terms of the agreement can spoil the peace process by unilaterally reigniting armed conflict. In this manner, spoiler factions act as veto players in the negotiation and implementation of a peace agreement.

Stephen Stedman argues that strategies for preventing spoilers from disrupting the peace process vary depending on the type of spoiler.[123] Some spoilers accept the idea of a negotiated settlement but will play the spoiler if the terms of the agreement are unacceptable to them. Such groups can be induced to join the peace agreement with further concessions. Extreme spoilers are factions that do not accept the legitimacy of the settlement process and prefer to continue fighting, presumably because they estimate that they eventually will be able to achieve victory. One strategy for dealing with such groups is to isolate them by brokering an agreement with the other factions, thereby building a large enough coalition in support of the peace agreement that the spoilers can be isolated and eventually subdued. It is reasonable to assume that civilians caught in the crossfire between rebels and government would prefer peace to continued conflict. There is a demonstrable war weariness effect in protracted civil wars. To the extent that mediators can forge an agreement that isolates the spoilers from the other rebel factions in the conflict, it may be possible to "win the hearts and minds" of the spoiler's civilian support base by persuading them that they would be better off by supporting the peace agreement and withdrawing their support from the spoiler faction than by continuing to support the spoiler faction and prolonging their exposure as targets of armed conflict. The spoiler's civilian support base can be won over more easily following the negotiated settlement because the settlement itself shifts the balance of power between state and rebels in favor of the state. The spoiler faction now has fewer allies in the conflict and the state has fewer rebel groups with which to contend. In this manner an extreme spoiler can be defeated by a peace agreement that induces its allies to defect and "drains the sea" of the civilian support base that is necessary for the spoiler to sustain its combat operations.

Peacekeeping Works.

Once a peace agreement has been negotiated, the success of its implementation can be enhanced considerably by the introduction of peacekeeping forces, especially under the auspices of the UN. UN peacekeepers have been deployed more than 60 times since the organization came into existence, and more than 45 of those have been deployed since 1985. The total cost of all 60 UN peacekeeping operations is about $60 billion. In several ways, this investment has been quite cost effective.

First, the promise of the introduction of peacekeeping forces makes it more likely that a mediator will succeed in getting the protagonists to agree to a negotiated settlement and that the agreement will be implemented successfully.[124] Walter has shown that the reason protagonists in a protracted civil war could not negotiate an end to the conflict on their own is not so much because the parties do not want to find a way out of conflict nor, primarily, because one or the other party objects to the terms of the settlement agreement. Rather, the major impediment to a peace agreement is that neither can afford to commit to disarming and demobilizing without some sort of third-party security guarantee.[125] As each protagonist disarms and demobilizes its armed forces, it becomes more vulnerable to possible violations of the peace agreement by its rival. The more vulnerable it is to its rival cheating, the less likely it is to fulfill its own commitments under the terms of the peace agreement. Therefore, the challenge in bringing about a peace settlement is not only how to devise acceptable settlement terms but also how to design a settlement that convinces both groups to let down their defenses and submit to rules of a new political game at a time when no government or police force exists to protect them from their rivals or guarantee their rival's compliance with the terms of the peace agreement.[126]

Peacekeeping forces provide the security guarantees that make it possible for both sides in a civil war to disarm and demobilize without fear of their rival's cheating on the agreement and achieving through deception the victory they could not achieve on the battlefield. Peacekeepers can verify compliance with the terms of demobilization, warn either side of a surprise attack by its rival, guarantee that soldiers will be protected as they demobilize, and take direct action if one or both sides resume combat activity. By providing a credible enforcement capability for the peace agreement, peacekeeping forces can thus ensure that the payoffs from cheating no longer exceed the payoffs from faithfully abiding by the settlement's terms. Once cheating becomes more difficult and costly, promises to cooperate gain credibility, and cooperation becomes more feasible for both sides.

Since protagonists in a civil war presumably are acutely aware of the problem of credible commitments and the ability of peacekeepers to resolve that dilemma, they are also more likely to agree to a settlement if the mediator promises to enforce its terms with peacekeeping forces. In this sense, the introduction of peacekeeping forces also tends to shorten the duration of civil wars.[127] And since the destructiveness of civil wars is more a function of their duration than of their intensity, the introduction of peacekeepers thus reduces the destructiveness of civil wars. Since the destructiveness of a civil war — in terms of both human casualties and damage to the nation's economy — is directly related to the likelihood of a nation experiencing a relapse into renewed civil war, peacekeeping forces contribute indirectly to the durability of the peace after a civil war.

A rather substantial and growing body of empirical research consistently confirms the positive effect of peacekeeping forces on the durability of the peace following civil war. Moreover, this same body of research confirms that this effect is not a matter of the UN "cherry picking" the conflicts in which it does introduce peacekeepers. Fortna, Gilligan and Stedman, and Svensson all show that, quite the contrary, the UN sends peacekeepers to the most difficult conflicts to resolve, and it mediates the most difficult conflicts as well.[128] More importantly, peacekeeping forces contribute substantially to the durability of the peace after civil war: peace agreements that are supported with peacekeeping forces are more likely to endure than those that rely on the former protagonists to sustain the peace on their own.[129] One recent study found that the introduction of peacekeeping forces reduced the probability of a relapse into renewed civil war by 70-80 percent.[130] Indeed, that same study found that, contrary to the "give war a chance" thesis, negotiated settlements supported by peacekeeping forces produced a more durable peace than government victories. The introduction of peacekeeping forces is the one policy manipulable variable that has the greatest effect on the duration of the peace after civil war (exceeding, for instance, the effects of economic development aid and democratization).[131] And this effect persists even after the peacekeepers have left.[132]

FROM PEACEKEEPING TO PEACE BUILDING

The impact of peacekeeping operations on the durability of the peace after civil war has been enhanced in the post-Cold War era by the evolution of a more robust and multidimensional approach to peacekeeping missions. Several post-Cold War peacekeeping operations have been endowed with the military capacity to go beyond simply supervising a truce to engage in more active forms of intervention in which the force compels the civil war combatants to stop fighting. Referred to as "peacemaking" operations, such operations have been deployed in Bosnia and Kosovo before the fighting stopped. Others have been charged with multidimensional peacebuilding responsibilities that include post-conflict institution building and economic reconstruction and rehabilitation. Besides disarming and demobilizing the former protagonists' armed forces, a number of the more successful peacekeeping operations have played a role in establishing and training a new army and a new civilian police force. They have supervised elections for the new post-conflict government, including building voter registration rolls, training election workers, managing the voting process, and counting the votes. Peacebuilding missions have been involved in rebuilding the bureaucratic capacity of the government to deliver basic public services and training the civil servants to staff those agencies.[133] "Second generation" peacekeeping missions have established post-conflict reconstruction and reconciliation programs and worked with nongovernment organizations (NGOs) to build the institutions of civil society that are vital to the successful operation and consolidation of democracy.[134] The success of UN peacebuilding operations in places such as Cambodia, Namibia, and Mozambique, to name a few, is indicated by the absence of renewed civil war, despite the fact that these were some of the bloodiest, most intractable and protracted conflicts of the last half century. Peacebuilding in this sense can substantially enhance the prospects for sustaining the peace in the aftermath of civil war.

Does Democracy Work?

The domestic corollary of the democratic peace proposition holds that democracies are less likely to experience civil war because the institutions and processes of democracy defuse revolutionary violence by providing opposition movements with peaceful, institutionalized means to pursue their interests and a reasonable chance to win control over (or at least influence in) government through free and fair elections. As noted earlier, several studies have shown that indeed democracies are less likely to experience civil war.

We would expect the same effect to hold in the aftermath of a civil war. The establishment of post-civil war democracy should make the peace more sustainable and reduce the prospects of a relapse into violent conflict. First, as noted earlier, opposition movements need not resort to organized violence against the state because they can pursue redress of their grievances through elections. Elected leaders have an electoral incentive to accommodate the demands of aggrieved groups in order to win their votes and thereby enhance their own prospects of victory at the polls. Second, democratic states are less likely to repress opposition movements because democracies usually contain institutional and constitutional constraints on the state's police power.[135] Moreover, elected leaders risk paying a price at the polls if they use repression against opposition parties, leaders, or their constituents. Because a democratic state is less likely to use repression against them, opposition movements (and their leaders in particular) are not compelled by the threat of state repression to choose between withdrawing from politics to avoid repression or adopting violent strategies of their own in order to combat it.

However, the evidence on the effect of democracy on the durability of the peace following civil war is not consistent. Doyle and Sambanis found some support for the proposition that both post-conflict democracies and the peace following a civil war were more likely to survive if peacekeeping forces were introduced following the termination of the civil war.[136] Walter found that when a full democracy was established in the aftermath of a civil war, the odds of a nation experiencing a new civil war (i.e., one involving new rebel groups) was less that 1/2 of 1 percent, compared to 2.5 percent for nondemocracies. However, she found no relationship between democracy and the likelihood of a relapse into war between the same factions that had fought the now-ended civil war.[137] Mason, Gurses, Brandt, and Quinn found some evidence that post-conflict autocracies and democracies were less likely to experience a recurrence of civil wars than are anocracies (i.e., weak authoritarian or semi-democracies).[138] However, Quinn, Mason, and Gurses found that post-civil war democracies are no more or less likely than nondemocracies to experience a resumption of civil war.[139]

The weak empirical support for the pacifying effects of post-conflict democracy may be a function of one effect discussed earlier: new democracies remain vulnerable to civil war. The vulnerability of new democracies to civil war is especially salient to the issue of sustaining the peace after civil war, since almost all post-civil war democracies are, almost by definition, new democracies. As such, post-civil war democracy remains fragile. While the logic underlying the preference for democracy (discussed earlier) is defensible, Roland Paris cautions us that democracy is based on the principle of competition and, in the immediate aftermath of a civil war, electoral competition can open old wounds, especially since the most likely basis for party formation is around the same organizations that were killing each other with considerable enthusiasm during the civil war.[140] Recent experience with civil war is not conducive to the level of trust required for good faith bargaining across party lines. Nor is it conducive to the willingness of losers in democratic elections to accept defeat and assume the role of loyal opposition. In new post-civil war democracies parties that lose elections have reason to fear that the victors will use the powers of office to attack them and diminish, through extra-constitutional means, the opposition's prospects for prevailing in future elections.

The fragility of post-civil war democracies may also be a function of variations in the institutional design of post-conflict democracies. Most scholars argue that parliamentary democracies are less likely to degenerate into civil war than presidential systems, and that proportional representation election systems for the legislature produce a more lasting peace than plurality/majoritarian election systems.[141] The preference for parliamentary systems is based on the notion that presidential elections are inherently zero-sum: the supporters of the losing candidates will perceive themselves to be excluded from the policy process. Certainly, they will have little if any influence over the most powerful officeholder in the government.

This can be dangerous for a new democracy that lacks the legitimacy that generations of effective performance and stable party institutions can confer on the state.

Proportional representation (PR) elections for the legislature — whereby parties are awarded seats in the legislature in proportion to the share of the vote they received — are preferred to plurality election systems because PR systems produce a more representative legislature. Minority groups are more likely to get representation under PR rules than under plurality elections, where each seat is awarded to the candidate with the most votes. Plurality election rules tend to produce "manufactured majorities," where parties can win a majority of the seats without winning a majority of the total national vote. Moreover, under plurality or "first past the post" electoral rules, ethnic minorities and new social movements have a more difficult time winning any seats in parliament because they have to come in first in a district to win a seat. Unless minorities are concentrated geographically so that they constitute a plurality in one or more electoral districts, they face the prospect of winning a smaller share of the seats than their share of the total vote.

The downside of the multiparty parliament that results from PR systems is that it is more difficult to assemble a stable governing majority when there is a high degree of party fragmentation in the legislature. When it takes two, three, four, or more parties to form a majority around any piece of legislation, it takes more time to get anything passed. Multiplayer negotiations have to take place, which delays the legislative process. What legislation does get passed tends to be more watered down, because the one means to get additional parties to join the vote for a piece of legislation is to drop from the bill those provisions that are unacceptable to that party. Thus, in a post-conflict environment where war weary citizens desire a government that can demonstrate its effectiveness by restoring order and reviving the economy, new democracies sometimes fail the test because of the difficulty of forming and maintaining an effective governing coalition in a legislature fragmented among multiple parties, many of which have a history of violent conflict with each other. For this reason, scholars such as Roland Paris and others advocate delaying elections until civil order and economic stability are restored, and a functioning government bureaucracy is in place to carry out the routine but essential tasks of government.[142]

Democracy requires mobilization — civil society — to counterbalance the power of the state. Groups that mobilize for democratic participation can also be mobilized for violent conflict. Democratic competition "works" only if all parties accept the rules of the game and assume (with good reason) that their rivals do as well. This is less likely in the fragile peace following a civil war. Democracy, as a form of what Przeworski has termed "institutionalized uncertainty," also requires that participants be willing to accept defeat, whether at the polls at election time or in the legislative process itself.[143] For democracy to survive — and for a post-civil war democracy to avoid collapse into renewed conflict — party leaders must develop a minimum level of trust in the fairness of elections, even when they lose. They have to be confident that if they lose one round of elections, they still have a reasonable chance of winning future elections. That level of trust in the operation of the institutions of democracy comes with experience with the successful operation of those institutions. Until that level of trust emerges, a new democracy's survival is at risk. As noted earlier, the failure of the peace following Angola's inaugural post-conflict elections in 1992 illustrates the fragile nature of post-civil war democracy.

Ethnic Divisions Matter.

Democratic competition can polarize society into hostile communities, especially when the basis of those communities is shared ethnic or religious identity. As alluded to earlier, armed conflicts that are grounded in ethnic or religious differences are especially intractable because the stakes—defined in terms of identity—are not readily divisible. When democracy is installed in ethnically divided societies, it often fails to inoculate the nation against the recurrence of civil war, and the empirical evidence supports this proposition. Mason, Gurses, and Brandt and Quinn found that all of the factors that contribute to a more durable peace after civil war—economic development, the presence of peacekeeping forces, democracy—still produced a less durable peace in ethnically divided societies.[144]

Democratic competition can, under some circumstances, exacerbate ethnic conflict. Donald Horowitz points out that in ethnically divided democracies, parties tend to form along ethnic lines, and this makes the consolidation of democracy problematic.[145] Any effort on the part of party leaders to form coalitions across ethnic lines or to forge multiethnic parties leaves them vulnerable to challenges from within their own ethnic group. The votes they hope to gain by making appeals across ethnic lines are usually fewer in number than the votes they stand to lose by being outflanked from within their own ethnic group by challengers who "play the ethnic card." With an ethnically based party system, elections can degenerate into little more than an ethnic census.[146] Minorities become vulnerable to the tyranny of an ethnic majority unless institutional protections are built into the constitution. While democracy requires that losers in elections accept their defeat, it also implies that they have a reasonable expectation of winning control of the government in a future election. If minority ethnic groups conclude instead that, because of their numbers, they are relegated to permanent opposition status, the payoffs from resuming conflict may come to appear more attractive than what they can expect to gain from accepting the status quo as the permanent opposition in an ethnic democracy. Sustaining a peace that denies them the prospect of ever leading a governing coalition can become less attractive than resuming an armed rebellion they see as offering hope for a better outcome through secession, revolutionary victory, or at least better terms in a new settlement agreement. Under these circumstances, an ethnic minority may resort to renewed armed conflict to challenge the dominance of ethnic majorities. Fearing this, the majority ethnic group may then feel justified in repressing that minority. An escalating cycle of repression and violence may ensue, culminating in a resumption of ethnic revolution or secession.

In Sri Lanka soon after independence in 1956, the Tamil minority found itself victimized by democratically enacted legislation that conferred advantages on the Sinhalese majority and institutionalized discrimination against the Tamil minority in such matters as admission to higher education, civil service positions, and officer positions in the military. A Sinhalese majority in the parliament even enacted legislation making Sinhalese the official language and favoring Buddhism over Hinduism (the religion of the Tamil minority). Tamil protests were met with communal violence directed against Tamils living in predominantly Sinhalese regions of Sri Lanka. The Sinhalese-dominated state did little to stop this violence. Eventually, Tamil youth became so alienated that groups such as the Liberation Tigers of Tamil Eelam (LTTE) gained enough support to sustain a secessionist insurgency. Attempts to resolve the conflict through negotiated settlement have so far proven fruitless.[147] Not surprisingly, most of the new post-Cold War civil wars that have erupted have been ethnically based conflicts, and many of them have occurred in new democracies that are deeply divided along ethnic lines.[148]

Economic Development Works.

There are strong reasons to expect that improvement in the rate of economic growth and development in a nation following a civil war contributes to a more durable peace. Presumably, a nation that experienced a civil war already had a weak economy; recall that the single best predictor of which nations will have a civil war is the level of income per capita. Civil war makes a weak economy even weaker by destroying infrastructure, productive capital, and human resources. It also encourages capital flight and disrupts commerce and production. Thus, a post-conflict environment is even less attractive to investors than that nation was before the civil war. The opportunity costs for participation in armed conflict were already low enough for a sufficient number of citizens to choose rebellion as an occupation over what the civilian economy offered. Years of armed conflict will only exacerbate these conditions.[149]

Therefore, a critical element of post-war reconstruction is for the international community to invest in rehabilitating the economy of a nation coming out of civil war. This does not necessarily require extraordinary amounts of assistance, in part because a war-devastated economy lacks the capacity to absorb large amounts of investment all at once. The marginal effects of even small amounts of investment are likely to be large, given the devastated condition of the economy. If the goal is to reduce the odds of civil war resuming, then the amount of external assistance and the form it takes should be geared to raising the level of economic well-being of the population as much as possible and as quickly as possible in order to raise the opportunity costs of participation in renewed conflict. Citizens with decent jobs and secure standards of living are less likely to risk that for the high risk, uncertain payoffs of joining a revived rebel movement.

Paris's "strategic liberalization" argument suggests focusing on stimulating economic growth and getting money circulating in the economy as quickly as possible. The typical austerity measures that the World Bank and International Monetary Fund have traditionally required as a precondition to receiving assistance are not appropriate in a post-civil war economy. They have the effect of increasing unemployment, raising prices and interest rates, reducing the purchasing power of people's earnings, and reducing the availability of public services. The economic hardship that results simply reduces the opportunity costs for participating in renewed armed rebellion. Austerity measures make it easier for aspiring rebels to mobilize popular support for a resumption of armed conflict. Likewise, privatization of state owned assets soon after the conflict has ended does not contribute to a durable peace. There are few locals with sufficient resources to purchase those assets. Selling them off in the immediate aftermath of the conflict is likely to result in many production units being shut down, throwing their workers into unemployment. This lowers the opportunity costs of participation in renewed conflict, making a resumption of civil war more likely. Instead, the immediate goal of post-conflict reconstruction should be getting people employed in the civilian economy so that they have less incentive to seek employment by rebel organizations or criminal organizations.[150]

CONCLUSIONS

The analysis of how civil wars end and what factors affect the duration of the peace after civil war suggests some strategies and policies that can contribute to, first, reducing the number of civil wars ongoing in the international system at any given time; and, second, building a more durable peace after civil wars end. The duration of civil wars is one feature of such conflicts that is most amenable to influence by policy interventions. As we have seen, protracted civil wars are "ripe for resolution." A credible third party mediator can broker a peace settlement that will bring such conflicts to an earlier and less destructive conclusion, compared to the alternative of letting them fight it out to a decisive military victory by one side or the other. The evidence across several studies suggests that such conflicts will *not* end in decisive military victory; they will simply continue on interminably, resulting in more deaths and more economic destruction, which makes that nation even more susceptible to a recurrence of civil war, should the current war ever end. Bringing a protracted civil war to an end by brokering a peace settlement reduces by one the number of ongoing civil wars in the international system. Moreover, by bringing civil wars to an earlier conclusion, negotiated settlements reduce their destructiveness, in human and economic terms, because the destructiveness of civil wars is more a function of their duration than their intensity. Since the destructiveness of a civil war is directly related to the likelihood of a nation relapsing into renewed civil war, settlements that bring civil wars to an earlier and less destructive conclusion also make the relapse into renewed civil war less likely. Thus, the first strategy for reducing the number of ongoing conflicts in the world is to mediate peace settlements to protracted civil wars in the Third World.

The evidence discussed suggests that the second cost-effective strategy for reducing the amount of conflict in the world is for the international community to target its conflict management resources on building a stable peace in nations coming out of civil war. The international community can do more to reduce the amount of conflict in the international system — the number of wars ongoing at any given time and the cumulative destructiveness of those wars — by investing in building a durable peace in nations coming out of civil war than by investing in early warning systems to prevent civil wars from breaking out in nations that have never experienced one. While we may be able to identify a set of nations that are at risk for civil war, we cannot predict which subset of those nations will actually experience the onset of civil war, nor can we predict when war will break out in any given nation in the risk set. Civil war is still a rare event even among the nations that are at risk. Whether or not a civil war does break out in an at-risk nation is, to some extent, a function of events within that nation (as opposed to structural characteristics of that nation that put it in the risk set), and those events (or "precipitating events") are not easily predictable nor readily manipulable by the policy instruments available to the international community. The intervention strategies required to inoculate *all* at-risk nations against the outbreak of civil war—e.g., substantial amounts of economic development aid and investment capital, programs to build state capacity and to ease the transition to democracy—would necessitate substantial investments of resources in a large number of countries. In some of those countries, the incumbent government would not be amenable to accepting such assistance even if the international community were to offer it because the reforms required to inoculate that nation against civil war would undermine the incumbent elites' control over political power.

What we are more certain of is that those nations that have had one or more civil wars in the recent past are far more likely to experience a relapse into civil war than any other nation in the risk set is to experience its first civil war. Therefore, a more cost effective conflict prevention strategy would target resources on building a durable peace in nations that have recently experienced civil war. This will reduce the rate of new civil war onset much more and for less investment than trying to build up the immunity to civil war among all impoverished nations with weak states (i.e., the complete risk set). To date, the wealthier nations of the world have not demonstrated any willingness to commit the level of resources to Third World economic development or Third World state building that would be required to immunize all at risk nations against the outbreak of civil war. Therefore, the more prudent and cost-effective strategy would be to target resources on preventing a relapse into civil war in nations that have recently ended a civil war.

Civil wars of long duration are "ripe for resolution." They have settled into a mutually hurting stalemate in which both sides recognize that their chances of prevailing over their opponent are rather remote. Under those circumstances, both sides should be receptive to an offer of third party mediation to broker a peace settlement to the war. Thus, the first step to reducing the number of ongoing conflicts in the world is to identify those that are ripe for resolution and initiate efforts to persuade the warring parties to agree to third party mediation of the conflict.

Brokering a peace agreement to such wars is the most likely manner by which protracted civil wars can be brought to a conclusion. Since the end of the Cold War, the international community has compiled a rather impressive record of success at bringing a large number of protracted conflicts to a peaceful conclusion through negotiated settlements. The result has been a decline in the number of ongoing conflicts in the world. The capacity of the international community, largely through the UN, to bring more conflicts to a peaceful conclusion by brokering settlement agreements could be enhanced if that capacity were more thoroughly institutionalized in the UN. To some extent, the success witnessed over the last 2 decades has been the result of a series of *ad hoc* efforts at mediation by the UN, individual member states, or groups of states. Encouraging as those successes have been, individually and cumulatively, that record suggests the possibility of even more success if the UN were to institutionalize the capacity to mediate peace settlements by establishing a new office devoted specifically to that task. Given that the total UN budget (including the cost of peacekeeping operations) is about $10 billion per year, the cost of adding such an office would be rather modest, especially compared to, say, the cost to the United States of prosecuting the war in Iraq.

After a civil war ends, the challenge becomes how to build a more sustainable peace. The research reviewed points to some policy options by which a more durable peace can be constructed, with a minimal investment of resources on the part of the international community. First, peacekeeping works. The introduction of peacekeeping forces tends to shorten the duration of civil wars because the protagonists are more likely to agree to a settlement if they have assurances of peacekeepers to enforce its terms. Shortening civil wars reduces their cumulative destructiveness because their destructiveness is more a function of how long they last than of how intense they are. In the absence of peacekeeping forces and third party mediation, the conflict would, in all likelihood, have lapsed into an interminable mutually hurting stalemate.

A further benefit of peacekeeping forces is that their presence reduces the likelihood that the nation will experience a relapse into civil war. Indeed, Mason, Gurses, Brandt, and Quinn found that the introduction of peacekeeping forces was the single most effective policy manipulable variable for extending the duration of the peace after civil war, reducing the probability of the peace failing in a given year by 70 percent.[151] Peace agreements that are supported with peacekeeping forces are more likely to endure than those that rely on the former protagonists to sustain the peace on their own. This peacekeeping effect is even more durable when the mission involves enough troops to deter an early resumption of conflict by one or both of the protagonists. And it is more likely to endure following missions that go beyond simply policing a truce to include assistance in building the institutions of a new post-conflict government, financial and technical support of economic reconstruction, monitoring elections for the new government, and providing assistance in demobilizing the troops of the former combatants and organizing and training a new unified national army and police force. The effect of peacekeeping forces on the duration of the peace is rather robust across studies; it holds up regardless of what data set one uses, what statistical method one employs, or what model specification one chooses. This effect lasts even after the peacekeepers have departed.[152]

Given this, a strong case can be made for peacekeeping forces being a relatively cost-effective tool for resolving conflict, preventing their recurrence, and, thus, reducing the amount and destructiveness of armed conflict in the international system at any given time. Since its creation in 1944, the UN has deployed more than 60 peacekeeping operations in various conflicts throughout the world. More than three-fourths of these missions have been deployed since 1985. Since the end of the Cold War, UN peacekeeping forces have been employed more than 40 times to enforce the peace following a civil war. They have also been employed to impose a peace where the protagonists could not be persuaded to put down their arms and come to the negotiating table, as in Bosnia and Kosovo. The total cost of all 60 peacekeeping operations is about $60 billion. By comparison, the United States has spent more than five times that amount in 4 years of fighting in Iraq.

The UN's record of success in the realm of post-civil war peacekeeping is quite remarkable. However, it seldom captures the attention of the general public because the very success of peacekeeping operations means that the mass media pack up their cameras and move on to the next conflict hot spot. Cambodia experienced at least three separate civil wars between 1967 and 1998 that resulted in more than one million deaths out of a population of only six million. Since UN peacekeepers were introduced in 1992, there has been only one brief resumption of armed conflict, and the maintenance of peace has made it possible for new democratic institutions to consolidate to a degree unimaginable in the 1980s. Likewise, UN peacekeeping operations in Central America sustained negotiated settlements to civil wars in El Salvador and Nicaragua, making it possible for those nations to embark upon the path to peaceful democratic development. Operations in Mozambique and Namibia have so far enabled those nations to sustain the peace and achieve levels of post-war economic growth that are unmatched by most of their neighbors in sub-Saharan Africa.

Investment in post-conflict economic development works. Because of the destructiveness of civil wars, the post-civil war environment is not a very hospitable environment for economic development. We cannot expect a thriving economy (or even a minimally functional economy) to spring up naturally from the ashes of civil war. International investment in post-conflict economic recovery and reconstruction is essential, not just for the host nation's economic health but as a peace-building measure as well. War weary citizens are less likely to support a call for the resumption of armed conflict if they have steady jobs, their children can go to school, and their standard of living is reasonably good and (perhaps more importantly) secure. Given the level of devastation that characterizes most post-civil war economies, the level of investment and aid required to jump-start the economy is relatively modest, especially considering the limited ability of those economies to absorb large amounts of investment. But investments geared toward generating employment and stimulating commerce, production, and consumption can put the nation on the path toward sustainable growth, which will make a resumption of civil war considerably less likely. Moreover, the level of investment required is, arguably, rather cost-effective, compared to the cost (to the host nation and to the international community) of renewed conflict. The UN operation in Central America (ONUCA) that enforced the peace following the Contra War in Nicaragua cost $92.4 million. The UN operation in El Salvador (ONUSAL) cost another $107 million. The total cost of the Central American peacebuilding operations is substantially less than the economic losses those nations suffered as a direct consequence of their civil wars. UN peacebuilding programs in Central America also cost substantially less than what the United States spent in military aid to defend the government of El Salvador and to aid the Contra rebels in their attempt to overthrow the government of Nicaragua. Peacekeeping operations in Mozambique and Namibia cost $492.6 million and $368 million respectively. None of these nations has experienced a resumption of civil war. Therefore, a strong case can be made that it is cost effective for the international community to invest in post-civil war reconstruction. Otherwise, the resumption of civil war becomes more likely and at a much greater cost—in human and material terms—to all involved.

In conclusion, social science research on how civil wars end and how to sustain the peace after civil war has identified a number of policy manipulable variables with which the international community can intervene to bring these conflicts to an earlier and less destructive conclusion, and to build a sustainable peace after the conflict has ended. All that is required is the political will and the institutional capacity to implement these strategies.

POST-SCRIPT: THE WAR IN IRAQ

The current public debate over U.S. strategy in Iraq is focused almost exclusively on two options: either increase the number of troops in order to achieve military victory over the insurgents (the so-called "surge"), or begin withdrawing U.S. forces so as to reduce American losses and compel the Iraqi military to "stand up" as U.S. forces "stand down." The research on how civil wars end suggests that neither of these options is likely to produce an outcome that either the United States, its allies, or the Iraqi government would consider favorable.

That research suggests that, at this point in the conflict, the surge by itself is unlikely to produce a decisive victory over the insurgents. It may reduce the level of insurgent violence in some locales for the short term, but it is unlikely to produce the sort of decisive military victory that would bring peace and stability to Iraq. Likewise, a withdrawal of U.S. forces by itself may reduce U.S. losses in the short term, but it will leave in its wake a weakened Iraqi regime in grave peril of disintegration in the face of an emboldened insurgency, unchecked Shiite militias, and foreign *jihadists*.

If the surge and the withdrawal hold little or no promise for a favorable outcome, what other options are available? Given what we know about how civil wars end (as discussed here), what is most puzzling

78

about the current debate is the absence of any serious discussion of the third option for ending a civil war: a negotiated settlement between the insurgents and the Iraqi government.

All civil wars end in one of three outcomes: a rebel victory, a government victory, or a negotiated settlement. We know something about the conditions predicting each of these outcomes. First, the longer a civil war lasts, the less likely either side is to win. If rebels win, they typically win early, more as a function of the implosion of a corrupt, inept, and illegitimate regime than of the battlefield prowess of the rebels themselves. If government wins, they too usually do so fairly early in the conflict because rebel movements start off at an overwhelming military disadvantage: they must build a rebel army from scratch in the shadow of a government that already has an established military. If rebels can survive their early military disadvantage, their ability to avoid defeat grows even if their ability to win does not. If neither side prevails within the first 4 to 7 years of the conflict, the odds are the war will simply settle into a mutually hurting stalemate, where neither side has the capacity to defeat the other, but both sides have sufficient strength to avoid defeat at the hands of their rival. In short, civil wars that do not end early in decisive victory tend to drag on interminably, bleeding the nation's population and destroying its economy. Contrary to Edward Luttwak's "give war a chance" thesis, protracted civil wars do not burn themselves out; they simply continue to burn.

Under those circumstances — i.e., a protracted mutually hurting stalemate — the most likely outcome (if the conflict is to be brought to an end) is a negotiated settlement, the one outcome that is not being discussed at present. The absence of public discussion of a negotiated settlement is especially puzzling because, since the end of the Cold War, more civil wars have ended by negotiated settlement than by a military victory by the government or the rebels. The *Human Security Brief* reports that in the 1990s, 42 civil wars ended in negotiated peace agreements, while only 23 ended in a military victory by one side or the other. Since 2000, the trend has been even more dramatic: 17 negotiated settlements and only four military victories. Thus, recent history suggests that, instead of arguing about whether to send in more U.S. troops or withdraw the troops that are there, we should be debating what steps can be taken to bring about a negotiated settlement to this conflict.

Achieving a negotiated settlement will be a daunting task, to say the least. However, at this point in the conflict, a settlement is no more difficult to achieve than a military victory. And the prospects for a negotiated settlement are far more encouraging than the prospects of peace and prosperity ensuing from a precipitous U.S. withdrawal. In short, a negotiated settlement is arguably the most attractive and feasible of the three options available at this point in time, and it should be at the center of the public debate on what to do about Iraq.

The Surge and Government Victory.

Four years into the conflict, the Iraqi insurgency has demonstrated that it has the force strength, tactical flexibility, and civilian support base to sustain its operations for the foreseeable future. Its persistence exemplifies the empirical trends discussed earlier: when governments defeat insurgencies, they most often do so early in the conflict. The longer an insurgency survives, the less likely the government is to defeat it. After more than 4 years of fighting, military victory by the government becomes a rather remote possibility, statistically speaking, and the Iraqi case offers little reason to expect a government victory at this point in the conflict. The U.S. troop surge may produce a temporary decline in insurgent attacks, but mainly in those areas where the troops are deployed. The insurgents will simply shift where they operate and what tactics they employ. In short, the surge is not likely to produce a decisive military victory. Indeed, in a study conducted by two political scientists at the University of North Texas (Andrew Enterline and Michael Greig), a series of simulations based on a statistical model of the survival of regimes imposed by foreign powers predict that the current surge in Iraq will have no effect on the likelihood of insurgency continuing. Interestingly, the same model predicts that, had the United States followed General Shinseki's advice and deployed 300,000 troops to stabilize Iraq immediately after Saddam Hussein was overthrown, the likelihood of an insurgency in Iraq in 2007 would be about the same as the likelihood of an insurgency in Japan 4 years after its defeat in World War II: near zero.[153] This too fits with the trends discussed earlier: if governments win, they win early. Thus, all indications are that, despite the U.S. troop surge, the Iraqi insurgency will survive, and the fighting will drag on. The conflict is likely to settle into a mutually hurting stalemate. The main value of the "surge" at this point is to enhance the bargaining position of the Iraqi government, should it choose to enter formal peace talks with the insurgents.

Withdrawal and State Failure.

On the other hand, the current state of Iraq's security forces does not inspire confidence in their ability to sustain the Iraqi regime if the United States withdraws its forces. A U.S. troop withdrawal would greatly imperil the survival of the current Iraqi regime. The Enterline and Greig study makes the same prediction: a withdrawal of U.S. forces will substantially increase the probability of the current regime failing.

Despite its democratic pretensions, the current Iraqi regime has not demonstrated the capacity to assemble an effective governing coalition that can address Iraq's many problems with effective policies enacted in a timely fashion. Its own base of popular legitimacy is fragile at best and eroding daily because the state has not demonstrated that it can deliver even basic services such as electricity, clean water, or (most critically) security from sectarian violence. The cabinet is paralyzed by the same sectarian and regional divisions that define the countours of the civil war. Those divisions preclude even the minimum level of trust that is required for factions in any democratic government to bargain with each other in good faith. It took months for the elected parliament even to choose a cabinet. In more than a year since, that cabinet has been unable to reach agreement on even the most fundamental question of how to divide up the revenues from Iraq's oil production. The parliamentary divisions that produce this *immobilsme* are intensified on daily basis by the continuing bloodshed between the hostile constituencies of rival parliamentary factions. This is not an environment in which the bargaining and compromises necessary for effective democratic governance have much chance to flourish.

No matter what level of training and equipment the United States has bestowed upon the new Iraqi army, it too is torn by the same tensions, hostilities, and distrust that permeate the government it serves and the society it is supposed to be pacifying. Recent history teaches us that new democracies sometimes do fail, even in peaceful societies.[154] The infant mortality rate among new democracies is even greater among those installed in the midst of a civil war. The protracted, bloody sectarian violence that dominates the environment in which the new democracy came into being greatly exacerbates all of the risk factors that work against the survival of a fledgling democracy. For these and other reasons, it is reasonable to predict that a withdrawal of U.S. forces from Iraqi would most likely lead to the failure of Iraq's democratic experiment through military defeat at the hands of the insurgency.

However, the overthrow of the Iraqi regime would not necessarily produce a new, more stable and effective (though decidedly nondemocratic) government for Iraq. The insurgency itself is fragmented among numerous armed groups, including several Sunni nationalist movements, composed largely of disenfranchised former Baathists and elements of the Saddam's now disbanded military. Al-Qai'da in Iraq and other foreign *jihadists* make up the second faction of the insurgency. Added to the equation are the several Shiite militias that oppose the Sunni insurgency but are not by any means under the command and control of the Iraqi government. While the current coalition of insurgent groups collectively might be capable of overthrowing the current regime in Baghdad (especially if U.S. forces withdraw and Shiite militias continue to operate free from government control), it is extremely doubtful that they would come together in unity to form a new, more effective (or legitimate) government that would be capable of establishing the order and stability that have eluded the United States and the al-Maliki government. The insurgents and the foreign *jihadists* are united only by their opposition to the U.S. presence in Iraq. Even if they bring about the disintegration of the current regime, it is doubtful they could subdue the Shiite militias. Instead, we can expect the fall of the current regime to be followed by continued sectarian violence as insurgent factions and Shiite militias battle among themselves for dominance in a now-stateless Iraq. Given the numbers, the level of organization and the firepower of both the Sunni insurgents and the Shiite militias, the level of violence in a stateless Iraq could escalate to genocidal proportions comparable to Bosnia. A stateless Iraq would be at risk of suffering through the sectarian equivalent of ethnic cleansing. Baghdad could be reduced to something resembling Beirut in the 1980s or Mogadishu after the fall of Siad Barre's regime in Somalia. The nation as a whole will become another stateless society on the order of Afghanistan after the withdrawal of the Soviet Union or Lebanon during the 1980s, only with oil reserves that will invite intervention by neighboring states. The power vacuum in Baghdad would destabilize the region; and Iran, Syria, Turkey, and Saudi Arabia would be tempted to intervene to prevent the rise of a new regime hostile to their own national interests. In short, the end result of a U.S. withdrawal would be another failed state crawling with competing militias, insurgents, and foreign *jihadists*. Iraqi citizens would be far less secure from violence with no more hope for a return to something approaching normalcy.

Negotiated Settlement: The Way out of War.

If military victory is unlikely and withdrawal is unlikely to produce a favorable outcome, what are the prospects for achieving and sustaining a negotiated settlement to the Iraq conflict? Achieving an agreement between the Iraqi government and the multiheaded hydra that is the Iraqi insurgency will certainly be no easy task. However, the research suggests that this third way is far more promising than either of the two options that dominate the current policy debate. The war in Iraq has been going on for 4 years. That means that Iraq has passed the point in the duration of a civil war where decisive victory by either the government or the rebels is likely. Instead, the most likely outcome for the foreseeable future is for the war to simply drag on.

The most feasible path to peace and stability at this point is for the international community to step in and mediate a negotiated settlement between the government of Iraq and the several insurgent groups as well as the Shiite militias. Evidence of the potential for success of this third way — negotiated settlement — includes the termination of some of the longest and bloodiest civil wars in the last half century. Civil wars in Cambodia, Mozambique, El Salvador, Nicaragua, Guatemala, Namibia, Sudan, Sierra Leone, and elsewhere have been brought to a conclusion by a negotiated peace agreement. Where those settlements have been enforced by UN peacekeepers, they have proven quite robust: contrary to Luttwak's assertions, the odds of the peace failing following a negotiated settlement that is supported by peacekeeping operations are lower than the odds of the peace failing following a government or a rebel victory.[155] There is no reason to dismiss this as a viable option for ending the civil war in Iraq, especially when the other two options are even less promising and potentially disastrous.

Third Party Mediation.

Getting to an agreement will be no easy task, to say the least, and features of the Iraq conflict make this task even more imposing. First, a third party mediator is needed; warring parties in a civil war are rarely able to reach an agreement on their own. Neither side can afford to trust that their rival will negotiate in good faith because each side has powerful incentives to misrepresent both their military capabilities and the terms of the peace settlement they would be willing to accept. Even if they could reach an agreement to stop fighting, disarm, and demobilize, both sides also have powerful incentives to cheat on the agreement in hopes of achieving through deception would they could not achieve on the battlefield. Thus, a third party mediator is necessary to resolve these commitment problems and make it feasible for the warring parties to reach an agreement by ensuring that the terms of the settlement will be enforced.

Who should serve as mediator? Despite criticism in the popular press, the UN has, in fact, compiled a rather impressive record of mediating settlements to civil wars since the end of the Cold War.[156] Moreover, this record of success at civil conflict mediation is *not* a function of the UN "cherry picking" easy conflicts to mediate; on the contrary, the UN takes on the most destructive, the most enduring, and the most difficult conflicts to resolve.[157]

The UN is especially well-suited to mediating the Iraqi conflict because, unlike the United States, the

United Kingdom, Russia, or any collection of regional powers, the UN does not have foreign policy interests of its own at stake in the outcome of the conflict. Generally, an effective mediator is one that can serve as a broker in working out the details of the agreement, and this requires that the mediator be able to make commitments that are perceived as credible to all parties involved in the negotiations. Nations that have their own national interests at stake in the outcome of the negotiations do not make effective mediators because the protagonists in the conflict cannot trust that the mediator will act to enhance the prospects for peace rather advance its own national interests, at the expense of the protagonists. This requirement would rule out the United States and the Great Britain as mediators in this conflict. Indeed, one of the most formidable barriers to a settlement will be persuading the United States to step back and allow the Iraqi protagonists to negotiate the terms of a settlement to their civil war without the United States attempting to dictate the settlement terms or assert a veto over specific provisions.

Second, reaching an agreement in Iraq is further complicated because the insurgency is fragmented among a number of indigenous groups and foreign *jihadists*, including al-Qai'da in Iraq. Further complicating matters is that the government has to contend with Shiite militias it cannot control. In short, this is not a simple two party negotiation. The more parties that are involved in the negotiations, the more difficult it is to construct an agreement that ends the conflict on terms acceptable to all parties. In effect, the more rebel groups there are, the more veto players there are in the peace negotiations and, therefore, the less likely the protagonists are to reach an agreement that can establish a sustainable peace.[158] However, getting Iraq on the road to peace does not necessarily require that all groups agree to a settlement. What is required is an agreement that incorporates enough of the insurgents and militias so that those who refuse to get on board are reduced to spoiler status in the peace process.[159]

The overwhelming majority of the insurgent groups are Iraqis, many of whom are former Baathists or military personnel. One can envision an agreement that would persuade those factions to reenter the political process and get out of the business of violent insurgency. Indeed, there is evidence of the willingness of Sunni insurgents to negotiate a peace settlement. Then U.S. Ambassador to Iraq Zalmay Khalilzad is reported to have met at least seven times in 2006 with representatives of more than 10 Iraqi insurgent groups. They presented Khalilzad with a Memorandum of Understanding on March 1, 2006, that suggested broad outlines for the terms of a negotiated settlement that would get them to lay down their arms and enter the political process. Although the terms were not made public, there are reports that the conditions would include:

1. Reform of the de-Baathification program mandated by the Iraqi Provisional Authority.

2. A national policy on the distribution of oil revenues.

3. Amnesty for the members of their insurgent organizations.[160]

In return, the insurgent leaders demanded a timetable for the withdrawal of U.S. forces linked to the buildup of Iraqi security forces, which would include reintegration of former soldiers and Baathists into those forces. The Bush administration may find these terms difficult to accept without political cover. However, these points could become the framework for a workable agreement that could provide the U.S. administration with the political cover to allow them to claim a diplomatic victory.

Settlement Terms.

What would the terms of a peace agreement include? If the goal of the negotiations is to bring the Sunni insurgents back into the democratic fold, then the agreement would have to resolve some of the very issues that the al-Maliki government has been unable to resolve on its own over the course of the last 2 years.

De-Baathification: First, undoing the extremes of the de-Baathification program would enable many Sunni insurgents and their civilian supporters to return to the jobs they had before the war. This would have the added benefit of restoring some of the technical expertise needed to rebuild the economy and keep the machinery of the government running smoothly, thus enhancing the new government's ability to provide the basic services that have been in such short supply since the U.S. invasion.

Getting an agreement on relaxation of de-Baathification reform and oil revenues is certainly feasible. Perhaps the promise of a peace settlement with the Sunni insurgents will provide the extra incentive to break the deadlock in the Iraqi parliament that has prevented resolution of these issues. With the UN serving as mediator in the peace talks, we can expect that both sides in the conflict—as well as the factions *within* the Iraqi government—might be more willing to consider a variety of proposals on these two issues because, with UN imprimatur, those proposals would not be perceived as somehow tainted by U.S. interests.

Oil Revenues: Second, some sort of agreement on the distribution of oil revenues among factions, regions, and contending groups in Iraq would have to be reached. There are certainly numerous models that could be used as a blueprint for this policy. Alaska, for instance, simply distributes revenues to citizens directly on a per capita basis. A similar plan in Iraq would have the advantage of injecting money into the economy from the grassroots, thereby stimulating consumption, commerce, entrepreneurship, and overall economic growth. This would also avoid the danger of parceling out revenues to the leadership of organized factions so that they could use those resources to fuel their own patronage machines, leaving average citizens with no access to the fruits of Iraq's petroleum reserves other than subordinating themselves to the patronage of local strongmen.

Disarming, Demobilizing, and Integrating (DDI): Third, disarming, demobilizing, and integrating former enemy combatants into a new national army is always the most difficult part of a peace agreement to implement. In Iraq, for the Sunni insurgents to buy into a peace agreement, it would also probably have to include disarming and demobilizing the Shiite militias as well. For this purpose, UN supervision of this project would probably be imperative. Neither the Sunni insurgents nor the Shiite militias are likely to agree to such a measure if the United States and its allies are involved in the DDI process.

Getting agreement on DDI that includes both Sunni insurgents and Shiite militias would probably require some sort of amnesty for members of both factions. It would also require a timetable for U.S.

troop withdrawal. While getting all parties to agree to these elements will be difficult, it will not be as difficult as achieving military victory or sustaining the current Iraqi regime in the absence of a peace settlement and 150,000 U.S. troops. The Bush administration has decreed no amnesty for insurgents who have killed American troops. That could be narrowed to apply to foreign *jihadists*. Without amnesty, the insurgents are not likely to agree to disarm and demobilize. History shows us that most successful counterinsurgency campaigns have involved amnesty offers to insurgent foot soldiers. This was a key element of President Magsaysay's program to defeat the Huk Rebellion in the Philippines.[161] Amnesty offers enabled the government of Thailand to undercut a communist insurgency there during the 1970s.[162] Amnesty will almost certainly be a necessary element of any settlement agreement that gets the Sunni insurgents out of the business of armed violence against the government. The further advantage of offering them amnesty is that reintegrated Sunni insurgents will become a valuable source of intelligence on al-Qai'da in Iraq and other foreign *jihadists* with whom the insurgents have been cooperating but with whom they have increasingly come into conflict over goals and tactics.

The other part of the peace equation is that the Shiite militias have to be part of the DDI program. Ostensibly, they are not part of the rebel opposition in the civil war since the government of Iraq is led by a Shiite majority. The most powerful and prominent Shiite militia, the Mahdi Army, supposedly answers to Shiite cleric Muqtada al-Sadr, whose party is part of the governing coalition. However, as long as these militias operate free of control by the government, the al-Maliki government will not be seen by the Sunni insurgents as a reliable negotiating partner in peace talks because his government cannot be counted on to deliver on any promises to guarantee the security of Sunni insurgents if they agree to disarm and demobilize. Indeed, any state that does not enjoy a monopoly over the control of coercive resources is not a fully sovereign state. Therefore, disarming and demobilizing the Shiite militias has to be part of the peace process as well.

That can best be achieved by a UN-managed DDI process, enforced by a robust UN peacekeeping force. Neither Sunni insurgents nor Shiite militias will agree to a DDI process that is implemented by either the U.S. military or the current Iraqi Security Forces. A UN peacekeeping force to replace U.S. forces would be more acceptable as a force to oversee the DDI program for both the Sunni insurgents and the Shiite militias. The UN has extensive experience in designing and implementing successful demobilization programs in civil wars in nations such as Mozambique, El Salvador, Nicaragua, and Cambodia.

UN Peacekeeping Forces: Finally, for the peace to hold, a multinational peacekeeping operation (led not by the United States but by the UN) would enhance the prospects of peace enduring. UN peacekeepers can enforce the terms of the peace agreement, assuring both sides that their rival's commitments under the terms of the agreement are credible because they will be enforced by UN peacekeepers. UN peacebuilding operations have also established a record of success at rebuilding political institutions and economic capacity in the aftermath of civil war. And the UN has a track record of setting up and managing elections for post-conflict regimes. It may be difficult to envision the Bush administration agreeing to a U.S. troop withdrawal as part of a peace settlement. However, if that withdrawal is part of a plan to replace U.S. and coalition forces with a multinational peacekeeping force, then withdrawal becomes not only strategically smart but politically feasible.

Dealing with Spoilers.

Of course, al-Qai'da in Iraq and other foreign *jihadists* are not likely to join in any such peace talks or sign on to any settlement agreement, no matter what its terms. But they should not be allowed a preemptive veto over the one option that, arguably, offers the best chance of bringing the civil war to a peaceful conclusion.

Recently, in Anbar Province, coalition forces have achieved some success at turning Sunni insurgents against al-Qai'da in Iraq. It is clear that the Sunni insurgents and foreign *jihadists* do not share the same goals in the conflict, nor do they always agree on tactics or targets. The split between them is being exploited with success in Anbar. However, the approach of turning one local insurgent group against al-Qai'da in Iraq and trying to replicate that process piece by piece across the entire nation is not a formula for a stable and lasting peace in Iraq. There is evidence that this strategy has been less successful in other parts of Iraq, including Baghdad. It does suggest that a comprehensive formal peace agreement with the Sunni insurgents is feasible, and that should be the goal at this point.

A peace agreement between Sunni insurgents, the Iraqi government, and Shiite militias would isolate the foreign *jihadists* from their Iraqi partners in violence. Al-Qai'da in Iraq would be left in the precarious position of being able to do little more than act as spoilers in the peace process. The defection of the major Sunni factions from the insurgency would also leave the foreign *jihadists* without any natural base of civilian support among the population of Iraq. At that point, the Iraqi people would face a choice: they can choose to continue to live their lives in the crossfire of armed factions by continuing to support a greatly diminished (and now largely foreign) insurgent coalition, or they can choose peace by withdrawing covert, overt, and even tacit support to al-Qai'da in Iraq and the other foreign spoiler factions. I suspect they will choose the latter. Once the spoilers are isolated, they will probably depart, and any remaining indigenous insurgents will eventually dry up as the sea of civilian support that is essential to the survival of any insurgency dries up.

However remote the prospects for negotiating an end to this conflict and building a sustainable peace, I would submit that those prospects are far less remote that the odds of the surge producing a military victory or the withdrawal of U.S. forces enabling the Iraqi government to restore peace and order on its own. Certainly, there are far more precedents over the last 20 years to give us hope for this third way than for any quest for decisive military victory over the insurgency. At the very least, given the gloomy prospects for the surge or the withdrawal, the prospects for brokering a negotiated settlement deserve entry into the center of the public debate on the war in Iraq.

ENDNOTES

1. The figures include 104 conflicts in the COW2 Intra-State War data set and four conflicts from the Extra-State data set: Morocco-Western Sahara, China-Tibet, Namibia, and India-Hyderabad. The COW data have not been updated past 1997. See Meredith Reid Sarkees, "The Correlates of War Data on War: An Update to 1997," *Conflict Management and Peace Science*, Vol. 18, No. 1, 2000, pp. 123-144.

2. The PRIO-Uppsala Armed Conflict Data Set can be accessed at *new.prio.no/CSCW-Datasets/Data-on-Armed-Conflict/ UppsalaPRIO-Armed-Conflicts-Dataset/*. See also the web-based version of the data set, with more details on each conflict, maintained by the Department of Peace and Conflict Research at Uppsala University: *www.pcr.uu.se/database/index.php*.

3. COW includes only conflicts that resulted in at least 1,000 battle deaths, whereas ACD adds those that resulted in as few as 25 battle deaths in a given year. See Nils Petter Gleditsch, Peter Wallensteen, Mikael Eriksson, Margareta Sollenberg, and Håvard Strand, "Armed Conflict 1946-2001: A New Dataset," *Journal of Peace Research*, Vol. 39, No. 5, September 2002, pp. 615-637; Lotta Harbom, Stina Högbladh and Peter Wallensteen, "Armed Conflict and Peace Agreements," *Journal of Peace Research*, Vol. 43, No. 5, September 2006, pp. 617–631.

4. See Harbom *et al.*, p. 617. ACD distinguishes between "intrastate conflicts" and "internationalized intrastate conflicts." The latter are civil wars in which the government, the rebels or both received military support from other governments. For the purpose of this monograph, we follow the conventional practice of treating both as civil wars.

5. Michael Doyle and Nicholas Sambanis, "International Peacebuilding: A Theoretical and Quantitative Analysis," *American Political Science Review*, Vol. 94, No. 4, December 2000, pp. 779-801.

6. Nicholas Sambanis, "What Is Civil War? Conceptual and Empirical Complexities of an Operational Definition," *Journal of Conflict Resolution*, Vol. 48, No. 6, December 2004, pp. 814-858.

7. James D. Fearon and David D. Laitin, "Ethnicity, Insurgency, and Civil War," *American Political Science Review*, Vol. 97, No. 1, February 2003, pp. 77-78.

8. Gleditsch *et al.*, p. 620.

9. Harbom *et al.*, pp. 618-619.

10. Fearon and Laitin, p. 77.

11. *Human Security Brief, 2006*, p. 7, *www.humansecurityinstitute. ca/images/stories/HSBrief2006/contents/finalversion.pdf*, accessed July 28, 2007.

12. *Ibid.*

13. Carolyn A. Hartzell, "Structuring the Peace: Negotiated Settlements and the Construction of Conflict Management Institutions," in T. David Mason and James D. Meernik, eds., *Conflict Prevention and Peacebuilding in Post-War Societies: Sustaining the Peace*. New York: Routledge, 2006, pp. 32.

14. Harbom *et al.*, p. 622.

15. "Structuring the Peace," p. 35.

16. Edward Luttwak, "Give War A Chance," *Foreign Affairs*, Vol. 78, No. 4, July-August 1999, pp. 36-44.

17. Fearon and Laitin, p. 83; Sambanis, p. 840; Paul Collier and Anke Hoeffler, "On the Economic Causes of Civil War," *Oxford Economic Papers*, Vol. 50, No 4, 1998, pp. 563-573.

18. Fearon and Laitin, p. 83.

19. Ted Robert Gurr, *Why Men Rebel*, Princeton: Princeton University Press, 1970.

20. Collier and Hoeffler, "Economic Causes," p. 568.

21. Henrik Urdal, "A Clash of Generations? Youth Bulges and Political Violence," *International Studies Quarterly*, Vol. 50, No. 3, September 2006, pp. 607-629.

22. Fearon and Laitin, p. 77.

23. Theda Skocpol, *States and Social Revolutions: A Comparative Analysis of France, Russia, and China*, Cambridge: Cambridge University Press, 1979.

24. Barry Buzan, *People, States, and Fear: The National Security Problem in International Relations,* Aldershot, UK: Wheatsheaf Books, p. 67.

25. Brian L. Job, "The Insecurity Dilemma: National, Regime, and State Securities in the Third World," in Brian L. Job, ed., *The Insecurity Dilemma: National Security in Third World States,* Boulder, CO: Lynne Rienner, 1992, pp. 11-35.

26. Jeff Goodwin and Theda Skocpol, "Explaining Revolutions in the Contemporary World," *Politics and Society,* Vol. 17, No. 4, December 1989, pp. 496-500. Goodwin and Skocpol use the term "exclusionary authoritarian regimes." Wickham-Crowley uses the term "patrimonial praetorian regimes" to characterize essentially that same syndrome of regime characteristics. See Timothy Wickham-Crowley, *Guerrillas and Revolution in Latin America: A Comparative Study of Insurgents and Regimes Since 1956,* Princeton: Princeton University Press, 1992, pp. 158-160.

27. H. E. Chehabi and Juan J. Linz, "A Theory of Sultanism 1: A Type of Nondemocratic Rule," in H. E. Chehabi and Juan J. Linz, eds., *Sultanistic Regimes.* Baltimore: Johns Hopkins University Press, 1998, pp. 3-25; H. E. Chehabi and Juan J. Linz, "A Theory of Sultanism 2: Genesis and Demise of Sultanistic Rule," in H. E. Chehabi and Juan J. Linz, eds., *Sultanistic Regimes,* Baltimore: Johns Hopkins University Press, 1998, pp. 26-48.

28. William Stanley, *The Protection Racket State: Elite Politics, Military Extortion, and Civil War in El Salvador,* Philadelphia: Temple University Press, 1996.

29. Jeff Goodwin, *No Other Way Out: States and Revolutionary Movements, 1945-1991,* Cambridge: Cambridge University Press, 2001, p. 45.

30. Stanley, ch. 1.

31. See T. David Mason, "Structures of Ethnic Conflict: Revolution versus Secession in Rwanda and Sri Lanka," *Terrorism and Political Violence,* Vol. 15, No. 4, October 2003, pp. 83-114.

32. Goodwin, *No Other Way Out,* pp. 46-47.

33. T. David Mason, *Caught in the Crossfire: Revolution, Repression, and the Rational Peasant*, Boulder, CO: Rowman & Littlefield, 2004, pp. 150-153.

34. Goodwin, *No Other Way Out*, pp. 47-49.

35. T. David Mason and Dale A. Krane, "The Political Economy of Death Squads," *International Studies Quarterly*, Vol. 33, No. 2, June 1989, pp. 175-198.

36. *Ibid.*

37. Mason, *Caught in the Crossfire*, pp. 155-156.

38. Nathan Leites and Charles Wolf, Jr., *Rebellion and Authority*, Santa Monica, CA: Rand, 1970, p. 91.

39. See Mason, *Caught in the Crossfire*; Mason and Krane; T. David Mason, "Nonelite Response to State-Sanctioned Terror," *Western Political Quarterly*, Vol. 42, No. 4, December 1989, pp. 467-492; Julia Heath, T. David Mason, William Smith, and Joseph P. Weingarten, "Calculus of Fear: Revolution, Repression, and the Rational Peasant," *Social Science Quarterly*, Vol. 81, No. 2, June 2000, pp. 622-633.

40. Goodwin, *No Way Out*, p. 49.

41. Fearon and Laitin, p. 85.

42. Leites and Wolf, p. 10.

43. Joel S. Migdal, *Peasants, Politics, and Revolution: Pressures Towards Political and Social Change in the Third World*, Princeton: Princeton University Press, 1974, p. 249.

44. Goodwin, *No Way Out*, pp. 49-50.

45. Fearon and Laitin, pp. 75-76.

46. Ted Robert Gurr, *Why Men Rebel*, Princeton: Princeton University Press, 1970.

47. Collier and Hoeffler, "Economic Causes."

48. Matthew Krain and Marissa Edson Myers, "Democracy and Civil War: A Note on the Democratic Peace Proposition," *International Interactions*, Vol. 23, No. 1, January-March 1997, pp. 109-118; Errol A. Henderson and J. David Singer, "Civil War in the Post-Colonial World, 1946-92," *Journal of Peace Research*, Vol. 37, No. 3, May 2000, pp. 275-299; Håvard Hegre, Tanja Ellingsen, Nils Petter Gleditsch, and Scott Gates, "Towards a Democratic Civil Peace? Democracy, Political Change, and Civil War, 1816-1992," *American Political Science Review*, Vol. 95, No. 1, March 2001, pp. 34-48.

49. See Timur Kuran, "Now Out of Never: The Element of Surprise in the East European Revolutions of 1989," *World Politics*, Vol. 44, No. 1, Ocotober 1991, pp. 7-48.

50. Hegre *et al.*, p. 42.

51. *Ibid.*

52. Fareed Zakaria, "The Rise of Illiberal Democracy," *Foreign Affairs*, Vol. 76, No. 6, November/December 1997, pp. 22-43.

53. See Brian L. Job, "The Insecurity Dilemma: National, Regime, and State Securities in the Third World," in Brian L. Job, ed., *The Insecurity Dilemma: National Security in Third World States*, Boulder, CO: Lynne Rienner, 1992, pp. 11-35.

54. ELF is calculated as $1 - \sum_{i=1}^{n} s_i^2$ where s_i is the group i's share of the population out of a total of n groups.

55. Collier and Hoeffler, "Economic Causes," p. 567.

56. Donald L. Horowitz, *Ethnic Groups in Conflict*, Berkeley: University of California Press, 1985, p. 37.

57. Shaheen Mozaffar, James R. Scarritt, and Glen Galaich, "Electoral Institutions, Ethnopolitical Cleavages, and Party

Systems in Africa's Emerging Democracies," *American Political Science Review*, Vol. 97, No. 3, August 2003, pp. 379-390.

58. Ibrahim Elbadawi and Nicholas Sambanis, "How Much War Will We See? Explaining the Prevalence of Civil War," *Journal of Conflict Resolution*, Vol. 46, No. 3, June 2002, pp. 307-344.

59. Ibrahim A. Elbadawi, "Civil Wars and Poverty: the Role of External Interventions, Political Rights and Economic Growth," presentation at the World Bank's Conference on Civil Conflicts, Crime and Violence, February 1999, Washington, DC; Marta Reynol-Querol, "Ethnicity, Political Systems, and Civil Wars," *Journal of Conflict Resolution*, Vol. 46, No. 1, February 2002, pp. 29-54.

60. Collier and Hoeffler, "Economic Causes," pp. 571-572.

61. Tanja Ellingsen, "Colorful Communities or Ethnic Witches Brew? Multiethnicity and Domestic Conflict During and After the Cold War," *Journal of Conflict Resolution* Vol. 44, No. 2, April 2000, pp. 228-249.

62. Lars-Erik Cederman and Luc Girardin, "Beyond Fractionalization: Mapping Ethnicity onto Nationalist Insurgencies," *American Political Science Review*, Vol. 101, No. 1, February 2007, pp. 173-185.

63. Fearon and Laitin; Collier and Hoeffler, "Economic Causes."

64. Ted Robert Gurr and Will H. Moore. "Ethnopolitical Rebellion: A Cross-Sectional Analysis of the 1980s with Risk Assessments for the 1990s," *American Journal of Political Science*, Vol. 41, No. 4, October 1997, pp. 1079-1103; Ronnie Lindstrom and Will H. Moore, "Deprived, Rational or Both? Why Minorities Rebel Revisited," *Journal of Political and Military Sociology*, Vol. 23, Winter 1995, pp. 167-190; James R. Scarritt and Susan McMillan, "Protest and Rebellion in Africa: Explaining Conflicts Between Ethnic Minorities and the State in the 1980s," *Comparative Political Studies*, Vol. 28, No. 3, October 1995, pp. 323-349.

65. Mason, "Structures of Ethnic Conflict"; Monica Duffy

Toft, *The Geography of Ethnic Violence: Identity, Interests, and the Indivisibility of Territory*, Princeton: Princeton University Press, 2003.

66. Scott Gates, "Recruitment and Allegiance: The Microfoundations of Rebellion," *Journal of Conflict Resolution*, Vol. 46, No. 1, February 2002, pp. 111-130.

67. Fearon and Laitin, p. 81.

68 Michael L. Ross, "What Do We Know About Natural Resources and Civil War?" *Journal of Peace Research*, Vol 41, No. 3, May 2004, p. 343.

69. T. David Mason and Christopher Campany, "Guerrillas, Drugs, and Peasants: The Rational Peasant and the War on Drugs in Peru," *Terrorism and Political Violence*, Vol. 7, No. 4, Winter 1995, pp. 140-170; on the more general relationship between lootable commodities and civil war, see Paul Collier and Anke Hoeffler, "Greed and Grievance in Civil War," *Oxford Economic Papers*, Vol. 56, No. 4, 2004, pp. 563-595.

70. Ross, p. 338.

71. James D. Fearon, "Why Do Some Civil Wars Last So Much Longer Than Others," *Journal of Peace Research*, Vol. 41, No. 3, May 2004, pp. 275-301.

72. Ross, p. 344.

73. *Ibid.* p. 346.

74. Fearon and Laitin, p. 81.

75. Humphreys, Macartan, 2003; "Natural Resource, Conflict, and Conflict Resolution," presentation at the Santa Fe Institute/ Javeriana University "Obstacles to Robust Negotiated Settlements" workshop, Bogota, Colombia, May 29–31, 2003, *www.santafe.edu/ files/gems/obstacles.* Cited in Ross.

76. Collier and Hoeffler, "Greed and Grievance."

77. Fearon and Laitin, pp. 85, 87.

78. Elbadawi and Sambanis, pp. 324–325.

79. Collier and Hoeffler, "Greed and Grievance."

80. Reynol-Querol, p. 39.

81. T. David Mason and Patrick J. Fett, "How Civil Wars End: A Rational Choice Approach," *Journal of Conflict Resolution*. Vol. 40, No. 4, December 1996, pp. 546-568.

82. T. David Mason, Joseph P. Weingarten and Patrick J. Fett, "Win, Lose, or Draw: Predicting the Outcome of Civil Wars," *Political Research Quarterly*, Vol. 52, No. 2, June 1998, pp. 239-268.

83. J. Michael Quinn, T. David Mason, and Mehmet Gurses, "Sustaining the Peace: Determinants of Civil War Recurrence," *International Interactions*, Vol. 33, No. 2, April 2007, pp. 135-165.

84. Karl R. DeRouen, Jr., and David Sobek, "The Dynamics of Civil War Duration and Outcome," *Journal of Peace Research*, Vol. 41, No. 3, May 2004, pp. 303-320; Patrick T. Brandt, T. David Mason, Mehmet Gurses, Nicolai Petrovsky, Dagmar Radin, and Patrick Macleod, 2005. "Never-Lasting Peace: Explaining the Duration of Civil Wars," presentation at the International Studies Association Annual Meeting, Honolulu, HI.

85. T. David Mason, Mehmet Gurses, Patrick Brandt, and J. Michael Quinn, "When Civil Wars Recur: Conditions for Durable Peace After Civil Wars," unpublished paper, University of North Texas.

86. Donald Wittman, "How A War Ends: A Rational Model Approach," *Journal of Conflict Resolution*, Vol. 23, No. 4, December 1979, pp. 743-763; Allan C. Stam III, *Win, Lose, or Draw: Domestic Politics and the Crucible of War*, Ann Arbor: University of Michigan Press, 1996.

87. Patrick M. Regan, "Third Party Interventions and the Duration of Intrastate Conflicts," *Journal of Conflict Resolution*, Vol. 46, No. 1, February 2002, pp. 55-73.

88. Stam, p. 34-37.

89. The following discussion of the model is based on Mason and Fett; Mason, Weingarten, and Fett.

90. Mason, Weingarten, and Fett.

91. The term "mutually hurting stalemate" was coined by William Zartman. See William Zartman, "The Unfinished Agenda: Negotiating Internal Conflict," in Roy Licklider, ed., *Stop the Killing: How Civil Wars End*, New York: New York University Press, 1993, pp. 20-36.

92. Mason and Fett, p. 560. See also Mason, Weingarten, and Fett.

93. Fearon, p. 276.

94. *Ibid.*

95. Barbara Walter, "Designing Transitions from Civil War: Demobilization, Democratization, and Commitments to Peace," *International Security*, Vol. 24, No. 1, Summer 1999, pp. 127-155.

96. Mason, Weingarten, and Fett, p. 261; see also Brandt *et al.*

97. DeRouen and Sobek.

98. Wickham-Crowley, p. 117.

99. Brandt *et al.*

100. Dylan Balch-Lindsay and Andrew J. Enterline, "Killing Time: The World Politics of Civil War Duration, 1820-1992," *International Studies Quarterly*, Vol. 44, No. 4, December 2000, pp. 615-642; Regan, "Third Party Interventions."

101. Patrick M. Regan, "Choosing to Intervene: Outside Interventions in Internal Conflicts," *Journal of Politics*, Vol. 60, No. 3, August 1998, pp. 754-779.

102. Patrick M. Regan, *Civil Wars and Foreign Powers: Outside Intervention in Intrastate Conflict*, Ann Arbor: University of Michigan Press, 2000, pp. 43-45. Fearon defines audience costs as "costs [that] arise from the action of domestic audiences concerned with whether the leadership is successful or unsuccessful at foreign policy." James D. Fearon, "Domestic Political Audiences and the Escalation of International Disputes," *American Political Science Review*, Vol. 88, No. 3, September 1994, p. 577.

103. Charles Tilly, *From Mobilization to Revolution*, Reading, MA: Addison Wesley, 1978, p. 200.

104. See Quinn, Mason, and Gurses.

105. Roy Licklider, "How Civil Wars End: Questions and Methods," in Roy Licklider, ed., *Stop the Killing: How Civil Wars End*. New York: New York University Press, 1993, p. 4.

106. R. Harrison Wagner, "The Causes of Peace," in Roy Licklider, ed., *Stop the Killing: How Civil Wars End*, New York: New York University Press, 1993, pp. 260-261.

107. Roy Licklider, "The Consequences of Negotiated Settlements in Civil Wars, 1945-1993," *American Political Science Review*, Vol. 89, No. 3, September 1995, pp. 681-690.

108. See Roland Paris, *At War's End: Building Peace After Civil Conflict*, New York: Cambridge University Press, 2004, pp. 63-69.

109. Quinn, Mason, and Gurses; Barbara Walter, *Committing to Peace: The Successful Settlement of Civil Wars*, Princeton: Princeton University Press, 2002. Doyle and Sambanis as well as Fortna include a "military victory" variable in their respective models, but in neither case do they look at the difference between rebel victory and government victory, and in neither case is "outcome" (i.e., victory versus settlement) at the core of their theoretical argument. See Paige Fortna, "Does Peacekeeping Keep the Peace? International Intervention and the Duration of Peace after Civil War," *International Studies Quarterly*, Vol. 48, No. 2, June 2004, pp. 269-292.

110. On changes in the political opportunity structure and their impact on social movements, see Doug McAdam, "Conceptual Origins, Current Problems, Future Directions," in Doug McAdam,

John D. McCarthy, and Mayer N. Zald, eds., *Comparative Perspectives on Social Movements: Political Opportunities, Mobilizing Structures, and Cultural Framings*, Cambridge, UK: Cambridge University Press, 1996, pp. 23-40.

111. Quinn, Mason and Gurses, p. 152.

112. *Ibid.*, p. 154.

113. Mason, Gurses, Brandt, and Quinn, p. 21.

114. Walter, "Designing Transitions"; Walter, *Committing to Peace*; see also Isak Svensson, "Bargaining, Bias, and Peace Brokers: How Rebels Commit to Peace," *Journal of Peace Research*, Vol. 44, No. 2, March 2007, pp. 177–194; Matthew Hoddie and Carolyn Hartzell, "Civil War Settlements and the Implementation of Military Power-Sharing Arrangements," *Journal of Peace Research*, Vol. 40, No. 3, May 2003, pp. 303–320.

115. Walter, *Committing to Peace*, p. 72; Svensson, p. 179.

116. Jacob Bercovitch and Karl DeRouen, Jr., "Managing Ethnic Civil Wars: Assessing the Determinants of Successful Mediation," *Civil Wars*, Vol. 7, No. 1, Spring 2005, pp. 101-102.

117. *Ibid.*, p. 102.

118. Carolyn A. Hartzell, "Explaining the Stability of Negotiated Settlements to Intrastate Wars," *Journal of Conflict Resolution*, Vol. 43, No. 1, February 1999, pp. 3-22; Carolyn A. Hartzell and Matthew Hoddie, "Institutionalizing Peace: Power Sharing and Post-Civil War Conflict Management," *American Journal of Political Science*, Vol. 47, No. 2, April 2003, pp. 318-332; Caroline A. Hartzell, Matthew Hoddie, and Donald Rothchild, "Stabilizing the Peace After Civil War: An Investigation of Some Key Variables," *International Organization*, Vol. 55, No. 1, Winter 2001, pp. 183-208.

119. Hartzell, "Structuring the Peace," p. 45.

120. *Ibid.*, p. 46.

121. *Ibid.*, pp. 44-45.

122. David E. Cunningham, "Veto Players and Civil War Duration," *American Journal of Political Science*, Vol. 50, No. 4, October 2006, p. 877.

123. Stephen John Stedman, "Spoiler Problems in Peace Processes," *International Security*, Vol. 22. No. 2, Autumn 1997, pp. 5-53.

124. Walter, *Committing to Peace*.

125. *Ibid.*

126. Walter, "Designing Transitions," p. 134.

127. See Brandt *et. al.*

128. Fortna; Michael Gilligan and Stephen John Stedman, "Where Do Peacekeepers Go?" *International Studies Review*, Vol. 5, No. 4, Winter 2003, pp. 37-54; Isak Svensson, *Elusive Peacemakers: A Bargaining Perspective on Mediation in Internal Conflicts*, Ph.D. Dissertation, Uppsala University, Uppsala, SE, 2006.

129. Fortna, p. 123; Mason, Gurses, Brandt, and Quinn.

130. Mason, Gurses, Brandt, and Quinn.

131. See *ibid.*; Quinn, Mason, and Gurses.

132. Fortna, p. 284; Mason, Gurses, Brandt, and Quinn.

133. Paul F. Diehl, "Paths to Peacebuilding: The Transformation of Peace Operations," in T. David Mason and James D. Meernik, eds., *Conflict Prevention and Peacebuilding in Post-War Societies: Sustaining the Peace*. New York: Routledge, 2006, pp. 107-129.

134. Eva Bertram, "Reinventing Governments: The Promise and Perils of United Nations Peace Building," *Journal of Conflict Resolution* Vol. 39, No. 3, September 1995, p. 388.

135. Steven C. Poe and C. Neal Tate, "Repression of Human Rights to Personal Integrity in the 1980s: A Global Analysis,"

American Political Science Review, Vol. 88, No. 4, December 1994, 853-72.

136. Doyle and Sambanis.

137. Walter, "Does Conflict Beget Conflict?" p. 384.

138. Mason, Gurses, Brandt, and Quinn.

139. Quinn, Mason, and Gurses.

140. Paris, *At War's End*; Roland Paris, "Peacebuilding and the Limits of Liberal Internationalism," *International Security*, Vol. 22, No. 2, Autumn 1997, pp. 54-89.

141. Hartzell, "Structuring the Peace."

142. Paris, *At War's End*; Paris, "Peacebuilding."

143. Adam Przeworski, *Democracy and the Market: Political and Economic Reforms in Eastern Europe and Latin America,* Cambridge, UK: Cambridge University Press, 1991.

144. Mason, Gurses, Brandt. and Quinn.

145. Horowitz, p. 295.

146. *Ibid.*, p. 318.

147. See Mason, "Structures of Ethnic Conflict."

148. Wallensteen and Sollenberg.

149. James C. Murdoch and Todd Sandler, "Civil Wars and Economic Growth: Spatial Dispersion," *American Journal of Political Science* Vol. 48, No. 1, January 2004, pp. 138-151; Seonjou Kang and James Meernik, "Civil War Destruction and the Prospects for Economic Growth," *Journal of Politics*, Vol. 67, No. 1, February 2005, pp. 88-109.

150. Paris, *At War's End*; Paris, "Peacebuilding."

151. Mason, Gurses, Brandt, and Quinn.

152. Fortna; Mason, Gurses, Brandt, and Quinn.

153. Andrew J. Enterline and J. Michael Greig, "Surge, Escalate, Withdraw ,and Shinseki: Forecasting and Retro-casting American Force Strategies and Insurgency in Iraq," *International Studies Perspectives*, Vol. 8, No. 3, August 2007, pp. 245-252.

154. Adam Przeworski, Michael Alvarez, José Antonio Cheibub, and Fernando Limongi, "What Makes Democracies Endure?" *Journal of Democracy*, Vol. 7, No. 1, 1996, pp. 39-55.

155. Quinn, Mason, and Gurses; Mason, Gurses, Brandt, and Quinn.

156. Svensson, *Elusive Peace*.

157. *Ibid.*, *Elusive Peace*.

158. Cunningham; Desiree Nilsson, *In the Shadow of Settlement: Multiple Rebel Groups and Precarious Peace*, Ph.D. Dissertation, Uppsala University, Uppsala, SE, 2006.

159. See Nilsson.

160. Gareth Porter, "Politics: U.S. Weighed Sunni Offer to 'Clean Up' Militias," December 13, 2006, available at *ipsnorthamerica.net/ news.php?idnews=564*, accessed July 25, 2007.

161. Benedict J. Kerkvliet, *The Huk Rebellion: A Study of Peasant Revolts in the Philippines*, Berkeley: University of California Press, 1977.

162. Thomas A. Marks, "Thailand: Anatomy of a Counterinsurgency Victory," *Military Review*, Vol. 87, No. 1, January-February 2007, p. 35.